This is a book about taking control of your cancer rather than being controlled by it.

I can vouch for the fact that the views presented are written by a man of faith, experience, and wisdom.

There are no rabbit trails here that will take you to dead ends. Every piece of advice you are about to read leads to life and life abundantly.

From the foreword
by HAROLD G. KOENIG, M.D.
ASSOCIATE PROFESSOR OF MEDICINE AND PSYCHIATRY

AND

FOUNDER AND DIRECTOR OF
THE CENTER FOR THE STUDY OF RELIGION/SPIRITUALITY AND HEALTH
Duke University Medical Center

What other experts are saying about
A Reason for Hope ...

As a cancer surgeon, I am delighted to see an increased interest in the value of faith and hope to promote healing. I welcome *A Reason for Hope* for its clarity and wisdom and highly recommend it for patients and their loved ones.

MARCIA MONROE MOORE, M.D. FACS

As a cancer survivor, I highly recommend *A Reason for Hope* as one of the most important books on cancer survival available. It is a must-read for cancer patients as well as for the family and friends who support them.

JERRY ROSE, *cancer survivor*
PRESIDENT, TOTAL LIVING NETWORK

Dr. Barry's insights are truly from the heart of a caregiver who has a close walk with the Lord. In *A Reason for Hope*, we learn that what the secular world may consider as "miraculous" is merely commonplace for those who put their future in God's hands.

ROGER CARY
PRESIDENT AND CHIEF EXECUTIVE OFFICER, MIDWESTERN REGIONAL MEDICAL CENTER (ZION, IL); CHIEF OPERATING OFFICER, CANCER TREATMENT CENTERS OF AMERICA

I am a cancer patient. From the moment you are told that you have cancer, you must overcome the initial shock and begin to fight for your survival. This book is inspiring and motivating to me, as I'm sure it will be to all cancer patients. I believe that with prayer, a competent medical staff, and a positive attitude, I will overcome.

REMO D. PIAZZI, *cancer patient*
PRESIDENT, UNITED EDUCATORS, INC. (LAKE BLUFF, IL)

A
REASON
for HOPE

A
REASON
for HOPE

GAINING STRENGTH
for Your
FIGHT AGAINST CANCER

Michael S. Barry

LIFE JOURNEY®
Bringing the Message Home for Life

COOK COMMUNICATIONS MINISTRIES
Colorado Springs, Colorado • Paris, Ontario
KINGSWAY COMMUNICATIONS LTD
Eastbourne, England

Life Journey® is an imprint of
Cook Communications Ministries, Colorado Springs, CO 80918
Cook Communications, Paris, Ontario
Kingsway Communications Ltd, Eastbourne, England

A REASON FOR HOPE
© 2004 by MICHAEL S. BARRY

First printing, 2004
Printed in the UNITED STATES OF AMERICA
  3 4 5 6 Printing/Year 08 07 06

Interior and Cover Design: Greg Jackson, JacksonDesignCo, llc

Unless otherwise noted, Scripture quotations are taken from the *Holy Bible: New International Version®*. Copyright © 1973, 1978, 1984 by International Bible Society. Used by permission of Zondervan Publishing House. All rights reserved. Other Scriptures are taken from the *King James (Authorized) Version* of the Bible.

Library of Congress Cataloging-in-Publication Data

Barry, Michael S., 1952-
  A reason for hope : gaining strength for your fight against cancer / Michael S. Barry.
    p. cm.
  Includes bibliographical references and index.
  ISBN: 1-56292-214-9
  1. Cancer--Patients--Religious life. 2. Cancer--Religious aspects--Christianity. I. Title.
BV4910.33.B38 2004
248.8'6196994--dc22
                              2004008641

This book is dedicated to my wife, Kay; my daughters, Sara and Becca; and my sister, Peg. My hope is that what I have learned about life in Christ will enable you to rise above all of life's challenges, remembering that God is always for you and never against you—and that all things are possible through Christ who strengthens you.

I also dedicate it to the cancer fighters who have fought and continue to battle to live the life God has given them, and to the members of Hope Evangelical Presbyterian Church, Libertyville, Illinois, who have graciously allowed me time to research and write.

Lastly, throughout the writing I have remembered my mother, Rose, who died of breast cancer decades before I was ready to let her go.

Acknowledgments

As a first-time author, I had not been aware of how much help authors like me get from people behind the scenes. I am deeply appreciative of all of those who have worked long and hard to insure that the message of hope this book brings was helpfully edited, handsomely published, and fervently marketed.

My thanks to Keith Wall, author of the included study guide, *Your Life Journey*. It helps the reader integrate the message into his or her personal life experience. This, of course, is why I wrote the book in the first place.

My thanks to Dan Benson, editorial director at Cook Communications Ministries, who shared my interest in getting the book's message of hope to the wider Christian community and for insuring that a good book was made better.

My thanks to my literary agent, Les Stobbe, whose interest, encouragement and helpful suggestions gave me hope that I might find a publisher, as well as someone who, at its inception, shared the vision of the book.

My thanks also to Dr. Harold Koenig who wrote my foreword. Knowing how busy he is, I still cannot believe that he took the time to write it at all, much less put so much of his heart and mind into corroborating the book's message. An act of sheer grace.

I am especially grateful to Stephen Bonner and Roger Cary of the Cancer Treatment Centers of America in Zion, Illinois, for their commitment to insuring that the spiritual needs of patients are not overlooked. And to Rev. Percy McCray, director of Pastoral Care at CTCA, who is a good friend, capable mentor, and dear brother in Christ.

MICHAEL BARRY
Hope-Books.com

Contents

Take Control of Your Cancer

Take Control of Your Cancer

Cancer is a disease in which attitude is everything. Getting and maintaining the right attitude is critical for survival—emotional, spiritual, and perhaps even physical survival. Scientists are only beginning to discover how closely the mind and the emotions are connected to the body and its responses to disease. The right attitude, then, becomes literally a matter of life or death.

Having cancer can be a difficult experience even for persons with deep religious faith. For those struggling with their faith, however, the burden of this disease can be enormous. This book will help you to bear that burden—and it will increase your faith.

The diagnosis of cancer sends a clear message: Now is the time to get it right. This time in your life, right now, presents a tremendous opportunity. At no previous time has there been such pressure and urgency to make the changes that really matter—changes that you had always intended to make, but never got around to. The time to delay, to put things off, is over. Cancer has a way of riveting a person's focus beyond the many usual distractions and onto the important things. Don't waste this precious time experimenting—desperately grabbing at one thing and then another. This is the time to embark on a new path—the right path—and this book will help you find and stay on that path.

Dr. Michael Barry has worked in the trenches with cancer patients and their families for many years and knows how to provide spiritual guidance. He knows what this disease is like—the devastating effects it can have—and what works and what doesn't work. I can vouch for the fact that the views presented in *A Reason for Hope* are written by a man of faith, experience, and wisdom. There are no rabbit trails here that will take you to dead ends. Every piece of advice you are about to read leads to life and life abundantly.

Cancer doesn't have to devastate your life. There are many reasons why you should have hope—reasons most people aren't aware of, reasons you probably won't hear from your doctor and maybe not even from your pastor. The information presented in this little book will help normalize and neutralize the fear that accompanies this disease and replace your fear with hope, determination, and direction.

❋

This is a book about taking control of your cancer rather than being controlled by it; about fighting the cancer; about becoming assertive in your treatment. It is also a book about forgiving—forgiving others, forgiving yourself, and forgiving God. It will help you release the health-damaging, cancer-fertilizing anger and despair that drive many to their graves and redirect this emotional energy toward life and hope. Dr. Barry will help you want to live, fight to live, and understand what you have to live for. Following his advice may not only add years to your life, if that is God's will for you, but it will infuse life into those years. Don't let cancer rob you of the joy that God wants you to experience during this time.

Dr. Barry supports the view that it may be God's will for you to be cancer-free so that you can serve and glorify Him in your life. So this is a book about miracles—real people like you who were miraculously healed and given a second chance. I don't know if it's God will for you to be cancer free in order to glorify and serve Him, or whether it is His will for you to glorify and serve Him in your dying and death. I do know that it is His will that you bear this disease with a Christlike attitude to whatever end it takes you. We are all destined to die, and whether you live a few more years is less important than making the changes in attitude that can transform your relationship with God, with yourself, and with others so that you will become the person God created you to be. If you accomplish that, then it really doesn't matter how long you live or how soon you die.

❄

You will want to keep this book on your bedside table. Read a chapter before you go to sleep, and read another when you wake up in the morning. Take it with you to the doctor's office and read it as you wait. Take it to the hospital with you during your treatments. Let these words sink deep into your mind, body, and spirit—let them add to and boost the healing effects of surgery, chemotherapy, radiation, or whatever kind of treatment you are receiving.

Given what we now know about the impact of the mind on the body and the impact of the spirit on both the mind and the body, there is every reason to believe that *A Reason for Hope* will have a very positive effect on your life. Not only is it good advice from a purely scientific and medical standpoint, but it is also good advice from a spiritual standpoint. Grow spiritually and fight the cancer at the same time—you can't go wrong.

A *Reason for Hope* offers a lifeline—do yourself a favor and grab it.

Harold G. Koenig, M.D.

Associate Professor of Medicine and Psychiatry

and

Founder and Director of

The Center for the Study of Religion/Spirituality and Health

Duke University Medical Center

INTRODUCTION

A Reservoir of Strength

---❖---

IF EVER THERE WAS A TIME
TO GET IT RIGHT, THE TIME IS NOW.

A Reservoir of Strength

A biblical view of history is linear, not circular. According to the Bible, there is a beginning and an end; a time when God created the heavens and the earth and, following the Second Coming, a time when history as we know it will come to a dramatic close.

Most of us who embrace the Bible's teachings do not believe in reincarnation—the belief that there are repeated opportunities to transform ourselves into higher, more perfect, levels of humanity. On the contrary, Christians believe that there is but one life to live, and therefore the challenge is, with God's help, to "get it right." There are no second or third chances. With this in mind, I originally titled the manuscript for this book *Getting It Right*. Anyone confronted with cancer—either as a cancer patient or as the spouse, family member, or friend of someone challenged by this dreaded disease—knows that the time to "get it right" may be limited. If ever there was a time to get it right, the time is *now*.

But then I realized that the message from my heart goes beyond the importance of living our lives right. While "getting it right" is indeed an important theme of this book, I also want to tell you that you have a profound reason for hope—a deep reservoir of physical, mental, emotional, and spiritual strength to draw from as you go to war against the cancer that could otherwise destroy your life.

As a Christian pastor and chaplain at a cancer treatment facility, I have spent hours with cancer patients. I've listened to their stories and observations, reflected with them on their disease, helped them better understand the role their faith can play at this critical time, and prayed with them and their families. I've heard the tough questions cancer patients wrestle with:

"Why?"

"Why me?"

"What's God's will in this?"

"Will I die or survive?"

These are tough questions with no easy answers. But in these pages I will share with you the answers that have come to my heart as I've worked with men and women and young people engaged in the battle of their lives. These answers will help you re-engage your faith, re-energize your mind and body, and revitalize your hope. These answers will truly give you a reason for hope.

※

I do not pretend to assume that my perspective speaks for the entire Christian community. However, as a pastor who has spent an immense amount of time with oncology patients, I believe my viewpoint, shaped by the biblical witness, will provide significant help to you in your battle with cancer. My goal is to be an advocate for life, as well as for the One who has given us life. While I write primarily to readers who share my spiritual worldview, I sincerely believe that those who do not call themselves Christians will also benefit from these pages. I also trust that anyone suffering from a serious disease other than cancer will find the strategies to be encouraging and helpful.

I have been blessed to work as a chaplain at a wonderful Midwest cancer treatment facility where the miraculous is commonplace, where many come dejected and leave hopeful—and in many cases cured of their cancer. May these words encourage you, give you peace of mind and spirit, hope beyond measure, and—most importantly—by God's grace, a cancer-free future.

REV. DR. MICHAEL S. BARRY

Hope-Books.com

CHAPTER ONE

Are You Hopeful?

---◆---

EVERY FORM OF CANCER PRESENTLY
KNOWN TO MAN HAS BEEN SURVIVED.

Are You Hopeful?

God has designed our bodies to *self-heal.* If we cut a finger, the human body will normally perform in such a way that the blood will stop flowing and the wound, shortly thereafter, will heal.

The self-healing ability of the body and mind, however, appears to have a close correlation to our level of hope. When we cut a finger, our hope (our expectation of a positive outcome) is *now* based on having survived similar experiences. But that has not always been the situation.

Imagine the first time you cut your finger. You were terror-stricken until your mother came alongside and told you that you would be fine. Together with the calming effect of her words of hope, a kiss was applied, along with a Band-Aid, and your finger self-healed quickly. As adults we no longer need words of reassurance for cuts and scrapes, since our hope for healing is based upon past experiences.

Obviously, cancer is far more serious than a cut finger, but the role of hope in the healing process remains the same. Without hope, our healing is, at best, impaired or delayed. At worst, hopelessness can lead to premature death.

When we have no hope for healing, our mind and body react in accordance with our thoughts and feelings. A marriage considered to be hopeless will not likely survive. A parent-child

relationship that is considered hopeless will likely not experience the healing power of forgiveness and reconciliation.

Employees who believe they have no hope for advancement
or due recognition will, in all likelihood,
underperform or quit. Hopelessness is the
breeding ground for depression, despair,
and death. This appears to be true whether
we are considering the health of a relationship, the health of our spirits, or the health
our bodies. When we have no hope, the
body and mind begin to shut down in anticipation of death. Not only is this truth self-
evident, it is also biblical. Proverbs 29:18
(KJV) tells us, "Where there is no vision, the people perish."

The first time I saw this fellow he was hopelessly near death; the last time I saw him he was alive, strong, vibrant, and making long-term plans.

A *vision* is simply a manifestation of that which is yet to be.
I interpret the proverb to mean that when God's people lose
sight of acquiring the future He intends for them (among other
things, a healthy body), they will perish. As the apostle Paul
reminded us, "For everything that was written in the past was
written to teach us, so that through endurance and the encouragement of the Scriptures we might have hope" (Rom. 15:4).

One of the most vivid examples I have witnessed of hope's
life-saving power involved a thirty-year-old young man with
pancreatic cancer. Physicians at a prestigious cancer treatment
facility gave him six weeks or less to live. When I met him, his
eyes were a hauntingly deep yellow. His skin also showed the
effects of jaundice. He appeared frail, thin, and frightened.
Everything about his demeanor displayed an advanced stage of
hopelessness.

But when I visited him eleven (!) months later, he was a completely different man. Healthy and strong. Smiling and hopeful. Excited and animated. His markers were demonstrating control—and defeat—of the cancer within his body. Will he live at least four more years and join the thousands of people officially considered cancer survivors? I cannot say. All I can bear witness to is what I have seen: The first time I saw

When we have no hope, the body and mind begin to shut down in anticipation of death.

this fellow he was hopelessly near death; the last time I saw him he was alive, strong, vibrant, and making long-term plans. The difference? Hope!

His hope was triggered by the facts that:

- God had brought him to a hospital whose commitment is to *life and living*, not *death and dying*.
- He is surrounded by a team of professionals committed to *fighting cancer*—medically, nutritionally, psychologically, and spiritually. We fight cancer with every weapon available through modern science as well as with age-old weapons of faith: prayer, worship, compassion, and encouragement.
- Most importantly, everyone is going all-out to instill an attitude of hope in our patients. In other words, from the president of the hospital to the lowliest employee, *the people ooze hope.*

Much like adults who no longer worry about a cut on their finger, our patients come to believe in and anticipate the body's amazing ability to self-heal. Our years of experience of treating the whole person—body, mind, and spirit—have made our staff enormously hopeful. We try to communicate that hopefulness to our patients in every way possible.

❄

As a Christian, where do I find hope? Hope grows out of my Easter faith. Easter teaches us that there is

no despair so dark,

no moral failure so grievous,

no thundercloud so threatening,

no disappointment so great,

no future so bleak,

no news so grim,

no life in such peril,

that our good and gracious God cannot remedy through His power to heal, comfort, restore, reconcile, and redeem. Such is the reason that God came to earth in the form of Jesus Christ. He wants us to live and love. As His children, we are reminded that Jesus had a physical body like ours. "Since the children [of God] have flesh and blood, he too shared in their humanity so that by his death he might destroy him who holds the power of death—that is, the devil" (Heb. 2:14 NIV).

The Christian's hope is grounded in the reality of a God who wants us to live long, abundant lives. He so much wants us to live that He became flesh in Jesus to die for us—and in dying, He destroyed the source of death.

The Easter message is clear: God created us for life—abundant life on earth and eternal life with Him in heaven. In a sense, this is the conclusion of the whole Bible. His desire for us to live is confirmed by His life-giving and life-sustaining Holy Spirit, who dwells within the hearts of all believers.

The Holy Spirit is a living force within us and equips us to live the life God intends us to live. It is God, the Holy Spirit, dwelling within parents who seek out prayer for their sick children. It is God, the Holy Spirit, within believers themselves who call upon church

Can there be any doubt about the healing power of prayer?

elders to anoint them with oil and to offer intercessory prayers on their behalf (see James 5:14). It is God, the Holy Spirit, who brings hope and healing to those who are weary, worried, and sick.

Last spring I attended a Spirituality and Health conference sponsored by Harvard Medical School's Department of Continuing Education. As one might expect at such an event, the speakers were all extraordinarily intelligent and committed to being top-notch medical professionals. Others were there to help us better understand the relationship between the mind and the body, faith and healing.

One of the featured speakers, a former pastor and now a university professor, told how he had recently received a call from a family asking him to anoint their crippled child and pray for her healing. The little girl's legs had been "crooked" since birth.

The pastor had had no personal experience in what we might call "faith healing," but he was aware of the biblical mandate to anoint and pray for the sick. After anointing the girl with oil and praying for her healing, he stood up, and to his amazement, watched her legs straighten out before his eyes. By the power of God, this little girl is walking today.

Can there be any doubt about the healing power of prayer? Can there be any doubt about the importance of placing our hope for healing into the hands of a loving, living, all-powerful God?

I must disclose here that my education has led me to be skeptical of people who claim to be "faith healers." I have a Master of Divinity degree from a prestigious, though liberal, theological institution on the east coast. My doctorate came from an evangelical seminary on the west coast. Neither of them, to my knowledge, encourage students to engage in faith-healing activities. And unfortunately, history has proven many so-called faith healers to be little more than carnival acts preying upon the good intentions of anguished people. Yet the Scriptures clearly teach caring ministers of hope to anoint the sick with oil and pray for them. I have trusted God to give me the right words to say when my parishioners or patients are so very vulnerable. The last thing I want to do is cause harm to anyone by further wounding an already desperate child of God. However, the faith that I have in Jesus Christ and the hope I have in His desire to comfort the sick have led me to use all of the spiritual resources I have to serve His purposes of love.

One afternoon I was called at the church by a young man asking me to come to his home to pray for him. He had just received bad news from his doctor, and he wanted me to come before his wife returned home from work. When I arrived, he told me that his legs had grown increasingly numb over time. That morning an MRI had confirmed his fears: there was a tumor on his spine.

As you can well imagine, this young man was filled with fear. I anointed his head with oil and prayed for him. I asked God to heal him—not only for his sake or the sake of his wife and family, but also for the sake of God's kingdom. Healing would give this fellow all the more reason to praise and glorify the Father.

Nothing happened immediately. I put the lid back on my vial of oil. I gave him a hug. I returned to my car and headed back to the church, getting there around 3 PM.

The next day, the young man called and told me this story: Around 6 PM the previous evening (three hours after I had left), as he was watching television in his recliner, he sensed that his body was being "blanketed by warmth." He felt God's presence in the form of a subtle and quiet invasion of warmth. His reaction was a feeling of awe, mystery, and calm. The "blanket of warmth" enveloped him for about ten minutes.

He then touched his legs, and nearly all of the numbness was gone.

He then touched his legs, and nearly all of the numbness was gone. By morning, the numbness had totally disappeared. Shortly after giving me this report my friend underwent another MRI. The tumor was completely gone. The only remaining evidence was a small, barely noticeable spot on his spine where the tumor had once been and is no more. No doubt about it, God had healed him.

Herbert Benson, M.D., founder of the Mind/Body Medical Institute and faculty member at Harvard Medical School, relates the story of Barbara Dawson, who chose to team her faith with radiation therapy to treat a tumor on her jaw.

Eschewing surgery any number of specialists would have said was necessary for her survival, Ms. Dawson fought cancer with treatments she believed in: radiation therapy and another powerful method that has existed since the beginning of time but has often been disregarded by the medical community. She unflinchingly believed in her treatment decisions, in her medicine and caregivers, and in God's power to heal her if it was His will to do so.[1]

Barbara's unwavering faith in God's healing power, teamed only with radiation therapy, led to a successful outcome.

Even though the experts had doubts about the course she chose, Barbara's unwavering faith in God's healing power, teamed only with radiation therapy, led to a successful outcome. I encourage you to follow Barbara's example:

Believe unflinchingly in your treatment decisions, in your medicine and caregivers, and in God's power to heal you if it is His will to do so.

Here is what I want you to take away from this chapter and this book: Regardless of how sick you might be, there is good reason for hope. With God's help, it is entirely possible that you will be able to control and even overcome the disease commonly known as cancer. Why? Because, as we're about to see, there is no form of cancer on earth that someone has not survived. Let me say that again: *Every form of cancer presently known to man has been survived by someone.*

But there is an even more valid reason for hope: another reality known as Jesus Christ, God's Son, whose Spirit indwells all who believe in Him—including you, by His grace. By His very nature He is the divine comforter, the healer, the giver of life.

Your reason for hope comes in believing that:

- Hope is a necessary ingredient in your healing process.
- Without hope, your healing may very well be impaired or delayed.
- At worst, hopelessness can lead to a premature death.
- The source of our hope is a living God, whose Spirit urges us to live and love abundantly.
- The Word of God is true. As Hebrews 2:13–14 reminds us, Jesus Himself became like us and had the same experiences we are having. He did this so that by dying, He could destroy the one who has the power of death.

A PRAYER OF HOPE

Father in heaven, help me to have hope by surrounding me with hopeful people. Help me not to receive bad news as though it is the last edition, but rather as one piece of information afloat on a river of facts flowing into a hopeful future. Heal me, I pray, not for my sake or anyone else's, but for Your sake. And ground my hope in the reality of Your profound and enduring love for me and desire for my well-being. In the name of Jesus I pray. Amen.

---

1. See "Barbara Dawson's Miracle" in Herbert Benson, *Timeless Healing* (New York: Diane Publishing, 1996), 204-207.

CHAPTER TWO

Are You Afraid?

(Of course I am, you idiot!)

LEARNING OF YOUR CANCER IS A SHOCK,
NO DOUBT. BUT THERE ARE OTHER
SIGNIFICANT FACTS YOU NEED TO KNOW—
FACTS THAT CAN HELP CALM THE STORM
YOU'RE GOING THROUGH RIGHT NOW.

CHAPTER TWO

Are You Afraid?

(Of course I am, you idiot!)

I have had the privilege of ministering to hundreds of cancer patients, and I can safely say that every single one of them had one thing in common: *fear*. Upon learning that they had cancer, these people became afraid, plain and simple. All of them.

So if you have cancer—or any other potentially life-threatening disease—and you find yourself feeling fearful, you are in very good company.

Consider the biblical story about Jesus and His disciples sailing across the Sea of Galilee in what was probably a small boat, less than twenty-five feet long (see Luke 8:22–25). Suddenly a storm arose. We are told that huge waves broke over the boat so that it was nearly swamped.

"Teacher," the disciples called out, "don't you care if we drown?"

The Lord responded by quieting the sea. The wind and waves died down and with them the disciples' fear.

He asked them, "Why are you so afraid? Do you still have no faith?"

This story fascinates me. The disciples had seen Jesus perform miracle after miracle and heal a wide variety of diseases, including a man possessed by an evil spirit, a man with leprosy, a paralytic, Peter's mother-in-law who suffered from a severe fever, and a man with a withered hand. Yet suddenly they were worried about their own well-being. They had been witnesses to incredible manifestations of God's power, yet *right at the moment* that their own faith should have provided peace,

"Why are you so afraid? Do you still have no faith?"

assurance, and calm, they responded as if their prior experiences of God's power and grace meant nothing. Their faith vanished at the very moment they needed it most. Upon experiencing calamity, their faith went overboard, allowing panic, fear, anxiety, and distress to overwhelm them.

If the disciples could experience fear after all they had witnessed, I suppose we should not be too hard on ourselves when we experience intense fear and anxiety. Feeling fearful is human and understandable. It is important, though, to learn the lesson the disciples learned: Jesus was in the boat with them. He did not abandon them. He was there for them, and He is there for you. Calm down. Rest. Relax. Trust in God's gracious love and in His concern for your well-being.

Learning of your cancer is a shock, no doubt. But your diagnosis is only one part of the total picture. There are other significant facts you need to know—facts that can help calm the storm you're going through right now.

EVERY FORM OF CANCER HAS BEEN SURVIVED.

At the cancer treatment center where I serve as a chaplain, one of the greatest encouragements people hear from our medical professionals is this: *Every form of cancer has been survived.*

A Stage 4 cancer diagnosis does not presume that a patient has gone beyond a point of no return. Certainly, the more advanced the cancer, the more difficult it is to slow or cure. Yet, time and time again, I have seen people at the brink of death gain victory. Why some and not others? Not until we see Jesus face to face will we know the answers to such mysteries. As the psalmist reminds us: "God has decreed the number of our days" (Ps. 139:16, author paraphrase). I take this to mean that God alone knows how long any of us will live. The best medical professionals in the world do not know how long you or I will be on this earth. Only our gracious and sovereign God possesses that answer. But … because every form of cancer has been survived, then you indeed have hope of surviving the disease you are facing. To put it another way, at whatever stage of cancer you find yourself, someone at that stage has survived.

Within the medical community, cancer is no longer considered a fatal disease.

CANCER IS A CHRONIC, CONTROLLABLE DISEASE.

Within the medical community, cancer is no longer considered a fatal disease. Instead, it is a chronic disease alongside diabetes, asthma, and high blood pressure. Many types of cancer are controllable, if not curable. Therefore, there is no logical reason to panic or become overwhelmed by the news that you have been diagnosed with cancer.

Unfortunately, not everyone in the medical community knows all of the oncological advances that have been made. And sadly, some medical professionals continue to treat cancer as though it is a death sentence. This simply is no longer the case. I work in a cancer treatment facility where many of the patients come from other cancer treatment facilities. Many of them have been told by their doctors that they had no hope. That also is not true. Where there is life, there is hope.

GOD CONTINUES TO DO MIRACLES.

I would be guilty of spiritual malpractice if I suggested to you that everyone who gets cancer is healed, even if they receive the best treatment available. Unfortunately, that day has not come; not everyone will be a long-term survivor of cancer. However, I would be equally guilty if I didn't share what I have seen with my own eyes. I have seen the most desperately sick people completely healed of their cancer.

Doctors do not heal; they are simply conduits of healing.

On a regular basis, I witness amazing acts of God's power to heal, to the point where remission and cure are commonplace. I have seen it so often that I cannot help telling you about it. I invite you to believe it! God continues to do miracles, and if it is a miracle you need, perhaps God will grant one for you. Why not trust Him for one in your life?

One Friday afternoon I was preparing to leave the hospital when I met a patient who was being discharged. I asked her how she was doing. She flashed a big smile and said that her examination had just revealed no trace of her tumor. Several months before, the tumor in her lung had been eleven inches long. Now it was gone.

A man in my congregation was recently scheduled for surgery to remove a tumor in his stomach. He is a man of faith, and together we prayed for God to heal him. During surgery, the surgeons could not find the tumor. It had disappeared. Scientists and the medical community refer to this rare phenomenon as "spontaneous remission." It is rare, to be sure, but it does point us toward other miraculous cures by Jesus— and it offers all of us hope that perhaps we too might experience a miracle.

BEING AFRAID IS UNDERSTANDABLE.
BUT IT IS NOT HELPFUL.

Over the years much has been written about personality traits and disease. The studies and observations suggest that there are high correlations between emotional behavior and certain forms of disease, such as ulcers, heart disease, and various addictions. One of the characteristics common to many cancer patients is that they are not very expressive of their feelings. They tend to keep deep feelings of anger, fear, and resentment to themselves.[1]

Keeping your feelings to yourself has a debilitating effect on your immune system.

Find ways to express your fear by talking with friends, family, or medical professionals. Admit your fear. Accept its reality in your life, then get it outside of you. Keeping fear to yourself is understandable. You probably have felt comfortable keeping these and other feelings to yourself for many years, but right now in your life it is not helpful. Help yourself by letting it go. Keeping your feelings to yourself has a debilitating effect on your immune system.

One study by Dr. E. M. Blumberg and his colleagues at the University of California at Los Angeles investigated personality traits of male patients who were receiving treatment for inoperable cancer. Using personality traits to predict the patients' survival time, the researchers discovered that they could predict the medical outcome in 88 percent of the patients. The most important characteristic that coincided with a rapidly progressing disease was an inability to relieve anxiety or depression.[2]

Again, fear is understandable. But it is not helpful. Do not keep it to yourself; express it. Ask God to overcome it with His peace, just as Jesus calmed the violent storm on the sea.

SPIRITUAL RENEWAL IS NOT UNUSUAL DURING ONE'S FIGHT AGAINST CANCER. MAKE THE MOST OF THIS TIME.

Bud Evans, a parishioner of mine, taught me that getting cancer has "not been all bad." Bud explained that in the four years since he discovered he had cancer, his faith in Christ has become more important and his work in the church more meaningful. He told me that he has re-evaluated his priorities; spending more time with his dear wife and family now top his list. Bud learned to share his feelings and concerns with his wife and with a cancer support group in our church. Like the Velveteen Rabbit, Bud found himself becoming more "real."

Fear is understandable. Just don't forget that Jesus is in the boat with you.

Such personal and spiritual renewal is common among cancer patients. Don't be surprised if it happens to you. I encourage you to read the Bible, particularly Luke's gospel. As you may know, Luke was a physician who, more than the other gospel writers, shares stories about Jesus' healing ministry. Use this time in your life to reconnect with the Source of life, and be reminded of His power to heal, to restore, and to forgive.

THERE ARE HOSPITALS THAT TREAT CANCER AND
THERE ARE *EXCELLENT* HOSPITALS THAT TREAT CANCER.

As a pastor, I have served at a number of hospitals over the years. I have also been a patient in a handful of them. They are not all the same.

Some hospitals are friendly and patient-centered. In others, though, you feel like you are a number at best and an inconvenience at worst. I cannot fully explain why that is. My guess is that the staff at your local hospital are committed to doing the best they can to insure proper treatment. Yet some health-care facilities are better than others in terms of communicating empathy, concern, and the very best medical, spiritual, and emotional care.

My advice to you is this: If you have a choice, find a hospital that has created the best possible environment for healing to take place. After all, that is the best any hospital staff can do in light of the fact that doctors do not heal; they are simply conduits of healing. Doctors are critically important to the healing process, but they do not heal. They are part of God's team of healers.

While I believe the best environment for cancer treatment includes the use of chemotherapy, radiation, and other advanced protocols, these elements do not address the needs of the soul, which I have found to be critically important as well.

Patients often relate stories to me of the depressing atmosphere at their oncology treatment centers. Depression and despair. Long faces. Gloom and doom. *It doesn't have to be this way.* There are cancer treatment facilities where the air is vibrant with care, concern, and hope!

Places where faith-related ministries are available to assist patients and their families during the time of spiritual renewal that often attends chronic disease ...

Where emotional needs are regarded with compassion ...

Where patients are educated in ways to help themselves cope with anger, forgiveness, or stress ...

Where the needs of the soul are taken as seriously as the needs of the body.

If you are going to be in a hospital, don't you want to place yourself in the hands of medical professionals who are hopeful, helpful, and who fully expect good things to happen to you while under their care?

Many of the patients I meet have been to the most reputable hospitals in the country. Most tell me that the hospital in which I work is the finest hospital they have ever seen. As a part-time chaplain there, I think I know why. The staff is committed to being "patient-centered." They care about you as a unique, complex person with a wide range of needs. They are open to learn from their patients. This attitude has helped them create an environment of love, care, concern, laughter, and hope. Combine these qualities with a commitment to excellence in the scientific aspects of cancer treatment, and the patient experiences a hospital that "sets the standard" for health care.

❁

Are you afraid? Of course you are. Give yourself permission to be human. Fear is understandable. Just don't forget that Jesus is in the boat with you. You are not alone. The voyage will continue, and the waters around you will be made calm.

Your reason for hope comes in believing that:

- Others have survived the form of cancer you have. Perhaps you will survive, too.
- Cancer is both controllable and curable. There is no reason to believe that yours cannot be controlled or cured.
- Miracles happen. If you need one, perhaps you will experience a miracle, too.
- Fear is a normal response. But you can move beyond fear to trust in God's love for you.
- Spiritual renewal is real. Use this time to (re)connect with God through prayer, Bible reading, and honest discussions with other Christians.
- Cancer treatment centers do not have to be depressing, gloomy places. There are excellent cancer treatment centers that minister to the whole person.

A PRAYER OF HOPE

Father, instill in me a reason for hope. Bring, I pray, calm to the raging storms of my life. I am afraid of the cancer, but I am not afraid of You. Help me place my trust not in the well-meaning doctors, nurses, nutritionist, and clergy who attend my needs, but in You and You alone. Use them, I pray, as conduits of Your grace, and bring me the healing I know You will bring me if You so desire. I offer my humble prayer in the name of the Great Physician, Jesus Christ. Amen.

1. John Sarno, *The Mindbody Prescription* (New York: Warner Books, 1999), 134.

2. Herbert Benson M.D., *Beyond the Relaxation Response* (New York: Times Book, 1984), 79-80.

Does God Want You to Live?

BELIEVE THAT GOD IS WITH YOU
IN YOUR STRUGGLE.
HE IS ALWAYS FOR YOU
AND NEVER AGAINST YOU.

CHAPTER THREE

Does God Want You to Live?

I f you have cancer, you are likely filled with feelings ranging
from sheer fright to numbness and confusion.
Your mind is probably thinking all kind of thoughts,
including whether your disease is some sort of punishment or
judgment from God.

You might be entering treatment believing that this is going
to be the *last* chapter of your life and that you will soon be
meeting your Maker—that yours is a life God could have
extended but chose not to.

These thoughts and feelings, too, are common among
cancer patients.

You are not alone.

As I talk with cancer patients, one of our
most frequent conversations relates to
forgiveness. One particularly vulnerable
woman tearfully asked me to pray for her, to
ask God to forgive her and to help her get
her life straightened out so that she could
be healed. While her disease may have been directly or indirectly associated with traumatic experiences of her past or
lifestyle decisions she had made, this woman needed to hear
about God's attitude toward *all* disease.

Perhaps you do, too.

*Do not fall into the
trap of believing
your current disease
is caused by God.*

God is pro-life. From the minute Jesus began His public ministry, He healed people from a wide range of diseases. From the biblical point of view, there is no room in the kingdom of God for diseases of any sort; otherwise, Jesus would not have chosen to heal the diseased or bind up the broken-hearted. Instead, He would have walked by them, turned a blind eye to their physical or spiritual condition, and concerned Himself with other, more important matters. But He didn't. He never turned anyone away who came to Him in faith.

Jesus said, "I have come that they may have life, and have it to the full."

Do not fall into the trap of believing your disease is caused by God. I believe that illness is instigated by the author of sin, Satan, who comes to destroy and take what does not belong to him. As Jesus taught:

The thief comes only to steal and kill and destroy;
I have come that they may have life, and have it to
the full.

JOHN 10:10

God's desire for the world, and for all of us, is to remove the "death grip" that sin and evil have upon us physically, emotionally, and spiritually. Consider these passages (I have italicized certain phrases for emphasis):

Praise the LORD, O my soul, and forget not all his bene-fits—who forgives all your sins and *heals all your diseases.*

PSALM 103:2–3

They had come to hear him and to be healed of their diseases; and those who were troubled with unclean spirits were cured. And all in the crowd were trying to touch him, for power came out from him *and healed all of them.*

LUKE 6:18–19

When evening came, many who were demon-possessed were brought to him, and he drove out the spirits with a word and healed all the sick. This was to fulfill what was spoken through the prophet Isaiah: *"He took up our infirmities and carried our diseases."*

MATTHEW 8:16–17

At that very time *Jesus cured many who had diseases,* sicknesses and evil spirits, and gave sight to many who were blind. So he replied to the messengers, "Go back and report to John what you have seen and heard: The blind receive sight, the lame walk, those who have leprosy are cured, the deaf hear, the dead are raised, and the good news is preached to the poor. Blessed is the man who does not fall away on account of me."

LUKE 7:21–23

When Jesus had called the Twelve together, he gave them power and authority to drive out all demons *and to cure diseases,* and he sent them out to preach the kingdom of God and to heal the sick.

LUKE 9:1–2

Is any one of you sick? He should call the elders of the
church to pray over him and anoint him with oil in the
name of the Lord. And the prayer offered in faith *will
make the sick person well;* the Lord will raise him up.

JAMES 5:14–15

The problem many of us have regarding the relationship
between faith and health is that we tend to compartmen-
talize our lives. After all, we do live in an age of specialization.
For example, we expect the government to take care of the
poor or the Salvation Army to care for the homeless. Too few of
us realize the importance of our
personal involvement in providing
direct care to "the least of these."

*Three-fourths of U.S.
medical schools now offer
courses on the relation of
spirituality to health.*

Similarly, when it comes to our
own health care, we assume that a
physician should tend only to matters
of the physical body. We go to medical specialists who, for the
most part, have little concern for our spiritual welfare. We
rarely expect physicians to pray with us or encourage us to
include prayer- or scripture-based faith in our battle against
disease. That role is relegated to clergy.

It would behoove us to keep in mind that the separation
between physician and clergy, and between spirituality and
health, is a relatively recent phenomenon. Religion, medicine,
and health care have been closely linked for more than 8,000
years, and it is only within the past 5 percent of recorded
history that have they been separated.[1] Today, fortunately,
health care is beginning to cycle back to the more holistic
approach. Ten years ago, fewer than one-fourth of medical

schools in the United States offered courses on the relationship of spirituality to health; today, *three-fourths* of our approximately 120 medical schools now offer such courses. My guess is that twenty years from now, spirituality and health will once again be fully re-integrated into the medical care we receive.

But here's the inherent challenge: The scientific and medical communities move slowly. And the church often moves even more slowly. Because we have learned to be primarily dependent upon nonfaith-based medical advice, we often assume, to our detriment, that faith is not really part of the healing process: that it is all about X-rays, lab tests, pharmaceuticals, and ultimately our doctor's opinion about our future. In other words, when it comes to our bodies, we allow our doctors to play God.

Consider King Asa of Old Testament times: "In the thirty-ninth year of his reign Asa was afflicted with a disease in his feet. Though his disease was severe, even in his illness he did not seek help from the LORD, but only from the physicians" (2 Chron. 16:12). This passage suggests that King Asa, who died shortly thereafter, had made the fatal error of excluding God from the healing process. It does not suggest that "seeking the physicians" is a bad or unhelpful thing to do. It simply underscores the obvious: There is a difference between being a physician and being God. Many people, including many with religious backgrounds, have been trained to respond like King Asa who, even when his disease was severe, sought help only from his physicians.

For those who hold a personal faith in God, excluding Him from the healing equation simply is not wise.

Let me be clear: Asa's story does not teach us to forsake appropriate medical care. Indeed, we should consult and heed our health-care providers. But we would also be wise to heed recent research, which shows that in 75 percent of medical situations our beliefs can play a major role in healing physical ills.[2] Thus, for those who hold a personal faith in God, excluding Him from the healing equation simply is not wise.

❋

If a doctor were to tell me that I am likely to die within a certain time frame, I would reply, "How do you know this?" Doctors have opinions based upon certain scientific criteria including studies, statistics, and their professional experience. With all due respect, it ultimately doesn't matter what your doctor thinks. What matters is what God thinks.

I am not a statistic.

You are not a statistic.

I refuse to be lumped into a category.

If you and I place our hope in the sovereign God who defies human statistics, we just may defy the odds.

As a Christian, I am confident of this promise: "He who began a good work in you will carry it on to completion until the day of Christ" (Phil. 1:6).

Try something: Go back and replace the "you" in that verse with your own name.

Does God lie? Of course not.

Can you believe His promises? You bet you can.

It is my belief that Jesus, who bore your sins upon His body on Good Friday, longs to bear your diseases as well—today and forever. There is no room in His kingdom for cancer, nor is there room for it in your body. Believe that He is with you in your struggle. God is always for you and never against you. There is nothing that can separate you from His love: "For I am convinced that neither death nor life, neither angels nor demons, neither the present nor the future, nor any powers, neither height nor depth, nor anything else in all creation, will be able to separate us from the love of God that is in Christ Jesus our Lord" (Rom. 8:38–39).

It ultimately doesn't matter what your doctor thinks. What matters is what God thinks.

Will anyone live forever? Not this side of heaven. And as I pointed out in the last chapter, sometimes, for whatever reason, God chooses not to heal. In those cases we must simply trust that He is our sovereign Lord and Creator. We must cling to the knowledge that He wants us to live fully and joyfully every day that we are granted life. Everyone will indeed die sometime, but the comfort that Christians have is the fact that Jesus will come to bring us to Himself, so that where He is we may be also (see John 14:3).

Your reason for hope means believing that:

- God is a God of life and healing. From the minute He began His public ministry, Jesus Christ healed people from a wide range of diseases.
- We get sick because we live in a fallen, broken world riddled with sinfulness, including the consequences of poor choices we might have made. God's intention is to break the death grip of sin on our lives and restore us to wholeness. If He chooses not to heal, He wants our remaining days to be abundant—filled with joy and intimacy with Him.

- You must accept God's forgiveness offered through Jesus Christ and commit to cooperating with His power to break the grip of cancer on your life.

A PRAYER OF HOPE

Father in heaven, thank You for the life You have given me, and for the eternal life promised through Your Son, Jesus Christ. Take my disease away, O God, and draw it to Yourself along with my sins, my worries, and my fears. Lord, if You want me to live, help me learn what I can do to help You bring healing in my body. Bless and make wise my doctors and all who tend to my needs at this difficult time in my life. In Jesus' name, amen.

---

1. Harold G. Koenig, M.D., from an abstract contained in seminar material distributed at a conference entitled "Spirituality and Health: A Multi-cultural Approach," offered by Harvard Medical School's Department of Continuing Education, at which Dr. Koenig was a plenary speaker.

2. Herbert Benson, M.D., *Beyond the Relaxation Response* (New York; Times Books, 1984), 82.

CHAPTER FOUR

Do You *Want* to Live?

---❖---

MIRACLES HAPPEN ALL THE TIME.
NOT TO EVERYONE, NOT EVERY TIME, BUT WITH
SUCH REGULARITY THAT WE SHOULD ALWAYS
KEEP THE WINDOW OF HOPE OPEN SO THAT
WE DON'T THWART THE MIRACLE
GOD MAY INTEND TO BESTOW.

Do You *Want* to Live?

During Jesus' ministry, a lame man had been sitting for years beside the Pool of Bethesda. One day Jesus came across him and asked, "Do you want to get well?" (John 5:6).

Perhaps you do not think it matters whether you desire to be healed. It could be that you think your attitude has little or no impact on the healing process. But I believe Jesus had a very good reason for asking the lame man if he *wanted* to get well. God designed you and me with a distinct mind-body connection. Your mind and your spirit can exert strong positive or negative influence over your body's capacity to fight disease or recover from injury. If your mind is resigned to staying diseased, your body will likely oblige you. But if you *genuinely* want to be made well, your body, to the extent it is able, will marshal the necessary forces to help accomplish that goal.

All evidence points to this simple truth: Your attitude matters.

Much has been written about the mind-body connection. Most information about this God-designed phenomenon is not gleaned through "hard science," but rather through occasional experiments and years of clinical observations made by professionals, including oncologists, psychologists, and clergy. All evidence points to this simple truth: *Your attitude matters*. A positive outlook, built upon an unshakeable faith in God's love for you, opens vast possibilities for healing.[1] Conversely, it is possible that you may have allowed your mind and emotions (via stress, unresolved conflict, sour attitude) to actually contribute to your body's illness.[2]

Much about the mind-body connection remains mysteriously unpredictable. For example, we know that unmitigated stress can lead to heart disease or ulcers (among other illnesses), but not everyone who lives a stress-filled life develops heart disease or ulcers. We know beyond a doubt that using tobacco can lead to cancer, though not everyone who smokes develops cancer. Likewise, there is a significant correlation between our minds (our thoughts, attitudes, and emotions) and our bodies (immune system, blood pressure, nervous system). The connection is definite, though it is mysteriously unpredictable.

Perhaps cancer is mysteriously unpredictable because we are mysteriously unpredictable.

Perhaps one reason the mind-body connection is mysteriously unpredictable is that our mental and emotional responses to various situations are highly individualized. Not everyone responds equally to the same experience. Confronted with a certain situation, one person may be emotionally devastated, another might react calmly, and yet another may find it humorous. Perhaps cancer is mysteriously unpredictable because *we* are mysteriously unpredictable.

Another reason we know little about the mind-body connection may be because we are conditioned to trust only hard science—that which is measurable, predictable, and reproducible. See the problem here? God is neither measurable nor predictable. Further, our prayers do not always yield consistently reproducible results. Some prayers are answered in the

WHO DOES THE HEALING?

We need to be certain about who does the healing. This point cannot be overstated: The *best* any cancer treatment hospital or facility can do for you is provide:

- the finest in medical professionals;
- progressive therapies, including chemotherapy and radiation;
- creative and helpful alternative therapies, including cancer-fighting diet and nutrition;
- sensitivity to your emotional needs; and
- resources and help for your spiritual needs.

Ultimately, God is the creator of life and the healer of disease. The absolute best any physician or health-care facility can do for a sick person is to create the optimum environment for healing to occur. Health-care professionals, whether they realize it or not, are merely conduits of God's grace.

way we had hoped, and others are not. The lack of predictability frustrates us and tempts us to place our trust in medical science rather than in God.

Still, most medical professionals, pastors, and priests "honor the mystery." Medical science itself is not always predictable, perhaps due in part to the attitudes and emotional well-being of patients. So, whether we're considering medical capability or God's sovereign plan for us, we do well to remember these words: "'For my thoughts are not your thoughts, neither are your ways my ways,' declares the LORD. 'As the heavens are higher than the earth, so are my ways higher than your ways and my thoughts than your thoughts'" (Isa. 55:8–9).

✻

Even though hard science sometimes contradicts faith claims, much of the available research supports the inter-relatedness of faith and wellness, even as it relates to our immune-system function. Dr. Harold G. Koenig, a leading expert in the relationship between faith and healing, writes:

> A strong immune system can fight off bacterial, viral, and fungal infections, as well as decrease the likelihood of developing cancer and reduce metastatic spread if cancer develops. There are many mechanisms by which religion may both extend the length of life and enhance its quality and meaning.[3]

Assuming you agree that there is at least *some* connection between the mind and body, the question then becomes: How does this affect you and your disease? From a *preventative* standpoint, it may have nothing to do with you. Obviously, if you already have cancer, the issue of prevention is moot. However, what you think about your disease certainly does matter.

"For my thoughts are not your thoughts, neither are your ways my ways," declares the LORD.

If you believe that your cancer is a death sentence, your chances of beating the disease will be much lower than if you believe you can overcome it. If you do not believe you are going to live, medical progress will likely be an uphill battle of dubious outcome. Once your mind is made up to die, the results may very well be foreclosed.

In an attempt to diagnose one patient's overall attitude, I asked her, "What do you think will be the outcome of your treatment?"

"Oh, I *hope* the chemotherapy will work," she responded. "But I don't really think it will."

Her general demeanor was fearful and anxious. In fact, she went on to tell me that she expected to "spiral downward and ultimately not make it."

As respectfully as I could, I said, "Can you hear what you're saying? You have all of the windows closed relative to what God can do."

When I saw the woman the next day, her demeanor was completely different. She was smiling, cheerful, upbeat.

I reminded her that people who were in worse shape than she have survived cancer; that every form of cancer has been survived; that miracles happen every day; and that there was no reason to think a miracle wouldn't or couldn't happen to her. I pointed out that her negativity may very well be counterproductive. And I suggested that she open the windows of her belief system and allow for the possibility that God intends for her to be healed. I prayed with her and asked God to blow through the windows of her heart and mind, that she might lean upon His everlasting arms and trust Him to bring healing.

When I saw the woman the next day, her demeanor was completely different. She was smiling, cheerful, upbeat. All she had needed was the reality check: Miracles happen all the time. Not to everyone, not every time, but with such regularity that we should always keep the window of hope open so that we don't thwart the miracle God intends to bring us. Matthew 13 tells us that Jesus didn't perform many miracles in His hometown because of the lack of faith, or openness, of the people there. God wants us to live in faith!

The medical community can provide you with a wonderful, hopeful, and positive healing environment. One area in which

The will to live is the necessary factor in the healing equation.

they cannot directly help you, however, is with *your personal attitude* toward life. The best hospital in the world, along with the most capable team of medical personnel, cannot give you the will to live. This is *the* necessary factor in the healing equation. This needed component in the ecology of wellness rests within your body, mind, and soul.

To be sure, Christians should not fear death, so I am not suggesting that death is the worst thing that could happen. From a Christian perspective, dying without a personal relationship with Jesus is the worst thing that could happen to anyone. Yet it is God who gave you life. It is God who has sustained you every minute of every day since you were born. Even as the psalmist spoke to God, he speaks for us:

For you created my inmost being; you knit me together in my mother's womb. I praise you because I am fearfully and wonderfully made.

PSALM 139:13–14

God gave you your life. The question that needs to be answered is the most basic and most obvious: *Do you want to continue living the life God fearfully and wonderfully made for you?*

If you are undecided in your heart whether you want to live, and to endure the tests and treatment that await you, remember these wise words:

> For as he thinketh in his heart, so is he.
>
> PROVERBS 23:7 (KJV)

Your attitude about the whole process may, indeed, make more of a difference than you can possibly know.

Your reason for hope comes in knowing that:

- If you *genuinely* want to be made well, your body, to the extent it is able, will marshal the necessary forces to help accomplish that goal.
- Modern scientific research sustains the belief that there is a strong relationship between faith and wellness—between our bodies and our beliefs.
- Although current studies support a mind-body connection, much about it remains mysteriously unpredictable.
- Your attitude matters. To your family. To your friends. To God.

A PRAYER OF HOPE

Father, replace all of my pessimism with optimism, fearfulness with hopefulness. As Jesus healed the man with the withered hand, heal my withered attitude and fill me with hope, as well as a desire to meet You in the midst of my pain and worry. In Jesus' name, I pray. Amen.

1. Herbert Benson, M.D., *Beyond the Relaxation Response* (New York: Times Books. 1984), 88.

2. Bernie Siegel, M.D., *Love, Medicine and Miracles* (New York: HarperCollins, 1986), 112.

3. Harold G. Koenig, M.D., from an abstract contained in seminar material distributed at a conference entitled "Spirituality and Health: A Multi-cultural Approach," offered by Harvard Medical School's Department of Continuing Education, at which Dr. Koenig was a plenary speaker.

Why Do You Want to Live?

I COULD NOT MUSTER THE PHYSICAL AND
MENTAL STRENGTH TO FINISH THE RACE.
I QUIT — SO CLOSE TO THE FINISH LINE.
FOCUSING ON MY PAIN INSTEAD OF
MY GOAL HAD DEPLETED ME.

Why Do You Want to Live?

The last chapter asked the question, "Do you want to live?" Assuming you said yes, the next question becomes, "*Why* do you want to live?"

The answer will automatically crystallize your motivation for living. Motivation reinforces our desire to live and helps us overcome much of the discomfort associated with cancer treatment. If our minds are focused on a positive goal, we can achieve a balanced perspective toward pain and suffering. That is, we know exactly *why* we're enduring the hardship and difficulty associated with treatment.

Yet when I ask cancer patients why they want to live, I am often met with blank stares and shrugged shoulders. Occasionally, they will say something like, "I want to live long enough to see my grandchildren get married." Or, "I want to see my child graduate from college." Or, "I want to live long enough to make it to my eightieth birthday."

These are not unimportant goals. Goals are critically important to our overall health. Human beings seem to have an amazing ability to *will* themselves to live long enough to fulfill certain goals.

Having a goal is vital. But it is even more important that we set the right goals.

Over and over again, I've seen individuals meet their goals and then spiral downward after having met them.

Having a goal is vital. But it is even more important that we set the *right* goals.

One middle-aged woman told me she had no idea why or how she had gotten cancer. Upon further discussion, I learned that she had always wanted to live to be 50 years old. At age 51, she was diagnosed with cancer. When I asked her why she had chosen age 50 as her target, she told me that her older sister had developed severe health problems at that age. Is there a connection between our health goals and the reality we experience? It would seem so.

Why do I want to be healed? What is there in my life worth living for?

Focus on God healing you. Place in your heart of hearts your desire to be well. Set your mind upon the day when you will be cancer free and you likely will not experience the degree of pain and frustration that other, less-focused patients experience.

Years ago I used to run 10K races (6.2 miles) on a regular basis. Occasionally I would run marathons (26.2 miles). I learned that if I focused on my breathing and on completing the race, my body would function at a high level. I experienced pain and discomfort, but I simply refused to focus on them or allow them to distract me from finishing the race. By concentrating on my goal, I was able to minimize the pain and its draining effect on my body. I was able to "run through" the discomfort and complete the grueling distance.

Once, however, at mile 20 of a marathon, my foot began to hurt. I thought I had a blister, so I stopped and took off my shoe only to discover that there was no blister at all. But after starting up again, I could not muster the physical and mental strength to finish the race. I quit—so close to the finish line. Focusing on my pain instead of my goal had depleted me.

Ask yourself this simple question: Why do I want to be healed? What is there in my life worth living for? What is a strong motivating desire that will force me to focus on the future and not on the anxiety, worry, or discomfort associated with cancer treatment?

Please take a few minutes to write down your reasons. Complete the following:

I WANT TO WIN OVER CANCER BECAUSE …

_____

_____

_____

_____

_____

_____

Having a personal reason to win is strong medicine in itself. But here's an even better reason: The Bible teaches us that God created us in His image (see Gen. 1:27), that He knew us before we were born (see Jer. 1:5), and that He has created us for the singular purpose of glorifying Him (see 1 Cor. 10:31). Therefore, every day of our lives should be lived for the purpose for which God created us: *that we might live for Him and for Him alone.* Shouldn't our reason for wanting to live coincide with God's desire for our lives? Doesn't it make sense that if we want to optimize our chances for healing, our personal goals should be in harmony with God's goal that we glorify Him?

Which prayer-goal do you think would be more powerful in your healing process? (1) "Lord, please heal me so I can live to be 90 years old," or (2) "Lord, please heal me so I can live my life for You and You alone." There's nothing wrong with wanting to live to be 90, but desiring to live in order to serve and glorify God brings higher purpose to our prayers and greater motivation for willing the body to fight.

❈

I remember one woman, beautifully bald, sitting up in her bed during chemotherapy. She was weeping. Because of her cancer, she confided, she had come to know Jesus. Her tears were those of thanksgiving and joy, for her newfound goal was to live her life differently—in service to God. Now her compelling reason for living wasn't just to see her daughter graduate or to travel to a place she had always dreamed of seeing. *She wanted to live for God.*

As you fight your cancer, I believe the best prayer of faith you can pray is that God would heal you so that you might live for Him. It's the right, supremely ordained reason. It is unselfish. It is a holy demonstration of your faith in the healing power of the One who created you, who has sustained you, and who died for you. Why do you want to be healed? So that you might live for Him. What does it mean to live for God? To use your life—including your gifts, talents, money, and time—in service to Him. The Bible teaches us that to live is to serve:

Every day should be lived for the purpose for which God created us.

Whoever wants to become great among you must be your servant, and whoever wants to be first must be your slave—just as the Son of Man did not come to be served, but to serve, and to give his life as a ransom for many.

MATTHEW 20:26–28

If you and I did not want to serve, it would seem that we are of little use to God. Wouldn't you agree?

After all, your reason for hope lies in:

- Being highly motivated to live.
- Having the best motivation possible: to serve God.

A PRAYER OF HOPE

Father, give me a reason for hope, I pray. Help me to get my affairs in order, which has less to do with preparing for death and more to do with preparing to live and serve. Give me life, if it is Your will. Bring encouraging people alongside me during days I feel like stopping. By the power of Your Holy Spirit, who dwells within me, focus my mind upon victory through Jesus Christ our Lord. Amen.

Chapter Six

Are You Willing to Fight for Your Life?

---------- ❖ ----------

LONG-TERM SURVIVORS
UNDERSTAND THAT THERE IS
A TIME TO BE NICE AND GENIAL
AND A TIME TO BE
FORCEFUL AND OBSTINATE.

CHAPTER SIX

Are You Willing to Fight for Your Life?

Many of the patients I meet tell me something very sad: Their primary care physician has indicated, directly or indirectly, that they have no hope and time is running out. They've been told, "Go home and get your affairs in order. You do not have long to live."

I always ask if those are *really* the words the oncologist used.

Invariably, the answer is yes.

These may not be the exact words, or even the intended message by their doctors, but it is what the patients heard. Rightly or wrongly, the message they "hear" is that their doctors have completely given up on them, there is no hope, and time would best be spent preparing for the final stage of life.

If God is sovereign, then no one, not even a physician, can determine when a person has reached the end of his or her life. Only God knows when that will be. The best the medical community can do is offer generalizations about the "likelihood" of certain outcomes based on statistical projections.

You are not a statistic.

But this overlooks one very important fact: You are not a statistic. You are a human being who deserves to be treated with dignity and respect. And if God has blessed you with a desire to live for Him, He also is supremely capable of working the miraculous in your life. Not only does God love you, He has expectations as well. God expects you to cooperate with His grace by accepting His love and by being a good steward of your body—and in the case of cancer or other serious illness, good stewardship involves giving your body the medical treatment it needs.

The Scriptures consistently recommend diligence and trust as we respond to life's challenges. For example:

> We want each of you to show this same diligence to the very end, in order to make your hope sure. We do not want you to become lazy, but to imitate those who through faith and patience inherit what has been promised.
>
> HEBREWS 6:11–12

> His master replied, "You wicked, lazy servant!"
>
> MATTHEW 25:26

In any area of life, including our health, God does not want us to be lazy. Yes, He is our ultimate healer. But as part of His overall plan, He has provided us with doctors, hospitals and care centers, research, and an ever-increasing amount of medical knowledge. Good stewardship means trusting God, but also taking full advantage of what God has already provided us. So we have work to do. We must do what we can do to help Him help us.

God expects you to cooperate with His grace by being a good steward of your body.

Which paves the way to the significant question of this chapter: *Are you willing to fight for your life?* This is a question for you, not for your doctor or family members searching for treatment options. *You* must decide your response! And your response is vitally important, for as we have seen, oncologists and researchers confirm the high correlation between a strong fighting spirit and long-term cancer survival. There are, in fact, numerous studies illustrating the link between the commitment to fighting disease and life expectancy.

There are also studies that correlate emotions with survival rate. I recall one report that women breast-cancer patients who did not openly express anxiety, anger, or other emotions were more likely to die within the first year of treatment than were expressive, "feisty" breast-cancer patients. As early as 1952, cancer specialists noted the "polite, apologetic, almost painful acquiescence of patients with rapidly progressive disease as contrasted to the more expressive and sometimes bizarre personalities of long-term survivors."[1]

Fifty years ago, the role of most women in our society was (I'm sure you would agree) significantly more passive than it is today. Traditionally, most women were inclined to be "polite, apologetic, and painfully acquiescent" and typically unwilling to confront, challenge, and display aggressiveness. Not surprisingly, passivity was a common characteristic of those who did *not* survive their cancer.

Bernie Siegel, author of *Love, Medicine and Miracles,* details the personalities of people he calls "exceptional cancer patients"—another name for which is "long-term survivors."

Quite simply, Siegel writes, survivors have personalities that experience a range of emotions. They play hard *and* work hard. They are quiet *and* talkative … rigid *and* flexible … gentle *and* aggressive. In other words, long-term survivors understand that there is a time to be nice and genial and a time to be forceful and obstinate.

Oncologists confirm the high correlation between a strong fighting spirit and long-term cancer survival.

There is a time to keep thoughts to oneself and a time to express them. There is a time to be gentle and agreeable, but there is also a time to say, "No! I *refuse* to be painfully nice. I *want* to live, and I *intend* to live as long as possible. I will not give up or play by your rules! It is *my* life, and I refuse to give in. I will continue to trust God who created me; maintain a positive outlook; and seek all the medical care needed to prolong the quantity and quality of my life."

Patients who have a natural disposition to fight, who can reject passivity and summon up a resolute, tenacious attitude, are more likely to add days, months, and years to their lives.

A study of patients with malignant melanoma underscored the danger of being "too nice" and compliant. These patients tended to worry more about their loved ones than themselves.[2] This personality type is being referred to more and more as Type C (the *C* is for cancer). Another description for Type C is "chronic niceness."[3] Generally speaking, chronically nice people don't like to rock the boat. They don't like conflict or confrontation. They avoid doing anything that might make others feel uncomfortable.

A study of women with breast cancer yielded this conclusion: Those who responded to the initial diagnosis of cancer by displaying either denial or a fighting spirit fared better than those who stoically accepted their condition or responded with feelings of helplessness or hopelessness.[4] Women who bottled up their feelings—the hallmark of the Type C—were more likely to have breast cancer than benign lumps.[5]

I also meet many chronically nice male cancer patients. Just like their female counterparts, they are quiet, decent, hardworking, and devoted. And quite often, they are angry, hurt, and filled with rage growing out of uncontrollable circumstances. The circumstances are

Another description for Type C is "chronic niceness."

compounded by the fact that these men tend to keep their feelings to themselves—an ominous combination when battling cancer.

⁂

If there is indeed a strong correlation between passivity and shortness of life, it is tragic to think how many people have been told by their physicians to "go home and get your affairs in order." In order to avoid conflict, these patients do exactly as they are told: They passively go home, passively get their affairs in order, and passively lie down to die.

Let me be clear: There probably is no "cancer personality" per se. Every conceivable personality has contracted cancer, including strong and weak, lighthearted and serious, kind and mean, thoughtful and careless, talkative and taciturn. But evidence clearly indicates that the will to win and a spirit of positive expectancy are vital to the immune system—and that passivity, negativity, and stress all tax the immune system. Dr. Harold Koenig writes:

Dr. Alison Fife, a psychiatrist at Brigham and Women's Hospital in Boston, and her colleagues explored the historical background of research connecting emotional health, the immune system, and cancer. After carefully evaluating over seventy major research investigations on this fascinating aspect of the mind-body connection, Dr. Fife's team concluded there was ample evidence that chronic psychological stress and emotional illness did indeed play a role in weakening the immune system, which in turn appears to increase risk of thyroid disease, diabetes, cancer and cardiovascular disorders.[6]

Passive people usually do not fight. They withdraw. Shy people usually keep their feelings of anger, disappointment, and hatred to themselves. They do not share them. And holding in all of those negative thoughts and feelings makes us sick. Know anyone who fits this category? Do you? Your long-term survivability of cancer may be determined by your answer to this question.

❊

Not everyone wants to *fight* to live. In her book *Angels and Bolters*, Karen Ritchie, M.D., is careful to note that there are various approaches to chronic and/or potentially fatal diseases. In some instances, patients prefer to focus on developing relationships and support systems than on fighting cancer. To them, loneliness is "worse than cancer."[7] These patients recognize that establishing and maintaining a proper support system not only defeats loneliness but can also help them battle disease. There is growing evidence that cancer patients who have good personal relationships and social support tend to survive longer than those who are socially isolated.

What's more, a Canadian study of patients with newly diagnosed lung cancer revealed that the odds of patients dying within a year were greater in cases where social support was lacking. Studies of women with breast cancer have confirmed that women who receive lots of *emotional* support from their partner, family, friends, and doctors tend to survive significantly longer.[8]

Recently, as I entered the hospital room of a cancer patient, I found him in bed with his loving wife sitting beside him. I talked with him about the importance of having a "fighting attitude." He tearfully confided, "I am not the fighter in the family. She's the reason I am here. She took charge and made all of the arrangements."

If he turns out to be a long-term survivor, it may be due to the love of his wife, her desire for him to live, and her willingness to teach him the importance of developing a stubborn and strong-willed attitude toward cancer.

If God is sovereign, then no one, not even a physician, can determine when a person has reached the end of his or her life.

About 50 percent of the patients I know are in treatment because of someone else's initiative. They have friends or family members who refused to give up. The other half are fighters, either instinctively or because they have discovered important reasons for living. Your attitude has a significant impact upon your outcome. Are you willing to fight your cancer? Or are you going to go "gently into the night"? I pray you will fight—and that God will provide you with hope, courage, clarity of purpose, and assurance of His love for you.

Your reason for hope means:

- Understanding that if you want to live, now is *not* the time to be passive, lazy, or overly nice. It is time to fight.
- Committing yourself to becoming a long-term survivor by being respectfully assertive with your health-care professionals.

A PRAYER OF HOPE

Help me, Lord, to fight this disease. Help me to take charge of my medical care and treatment. Give me a positive, fighting spirit. Help me to say no when it is appropriate, remembering always to treat everyone, including the medical staff attending me, with the same dignity and respect that I expect of them. Guard me from the temptation to resign to passivity, negativity, or anxiety. Surround me with people who care about me and who will pick me up if I fall. In Jesus' name, I pray. Amen.

1. Pennebaker, 146-147.

2. John Sarno, *The Mindbody Prescription* (New York: Warner Books, 1999), 134.

3. www.cancerassistonline.com/Subscrip/Articlefolder/TypeC.htm.

4. Paul Martin, *The Healing Mind* (New York: Griffin Books, 1999), 230.

5. Ibid., 228.

6. Harold G. Koenig, M.D., *The Healing Power of Faith* (New York: Touchstone, 2001), 217.

7. Karen Ritchie, *Angels and Bolters* (New York: Xlibris, 2002), 90.

8. Paul Martin, *The Healing Mind*, 231.

What Can You Do to Help Yourself?

ONE OF THE GREAT JOYS
PATIENTS SHARE WITH ME
IS THAT OF BUMPING
INTO A DOCTOR WHO HAD
PREVIOUSLY GIVEN UP ON THEM.

CHAPTER SEVEN

What Can You Do to Help Yourself?

In previous chapters we have discussed essential principles necessary for your fight against cancer—the importance of maintaining hope, identifying specific reasons to live, and taking advantage of the God-designed mind-body connection. In this chapter, let's roll up our sleeves and look at six practical ways you can help yourself battle disease while simultaneously bolstering your spiritual and emotional reserves.

1. TAKE CONTROL OF YOUR OWN HEALTH CARE.

I regularly teach a class on Spirituality and Health at a cancer treatment facility. One of the most common feelings patients express is a "loss of control." They used to feel a sense of personal control over their lives, but now everyone else seems to be making decisions for them.

There are many possible ways to react to the news of cancer or any other serious illness. These range from complete passivity to complete control—from allowing the disease to follow its course to going all-out in opposition to the disease. In the last chapter I mentioned the insightful book *Angels and Bolters* by Karen Ritchie, M.D. In this book the author describes our reactions to life as our "life scripts." The script that many cancer patients choose is the "War Script." Here the patient perceives himself or herself as the "victim" and the doctor as the "general" who, hopefully, will be able to lead the battle against cancer to a victorious conclusion. The patient is committed to fighting cancer and equally committed to being a dutiful soldier who follows the general's orders.

Forgiveness is not only wise stewardship of your mind, body, and soul, but it is also your spiritual obligation.

While the War Script can be helpful in that the patient is resolved to fight, its inherent weakness is that the patient tends to wait for the doctor's orders while taking little initiative to ask questions, make pivotal lifestyle decisions, or pose alternative ideas. These are the "chronically nice" patients we saw in the last chapter.

Dr. Ritchie suggests a helpful alternative in which the patient assertively engages in all decisions related to his or her treatment and lifestyle. Ritchie calls this the "Take Control" script, which calls on the patient to virtually take charge of the fight. Taking control of your cancer means making the decisions about your health care because you believe it is in *your best interest* to do so, even if the decision process might hurt other people's feelings.

Of course, taking control quite often goes against the grain for many chronically nice people, who by nature are more likely to agree with whatever someone else wants them to do. The chronically nice do not usually challenge authority figures, especially physicians. Who, after all, wants to make their doctor angry?

But it is *your* life, not your doctor's. Be polite, but be firm. Give yourself permission to obtain advice from other medical professionals. Your doctor may not like it, but what matters is what *you* think.

One of the great joys patients share with me is that of bumping into a doctor who had previously given up on them (the one who had told them to go home, get their affairs in order, and wait to die). Long after these patients were told they would be gone, they are alive. Perhaps it is vindictive to delight in the doctor's embarrassment, but I heartily believe that laughing in the face of death is one of the benefits of being a person of faith. As the psalmist wrote:

> He who goes out weeping, carrying seed to sow, will return with songs of joy, carrying sheaves with him.
>
> PSALM 126:6

2. Forgive those who have hurt you, including your doctors.

Patients whose doctors have given up on them often harbor anger toward those professionals. And sometimes this is an understatement. I remember one burly man who seethed with anger toward his doctor who, he believed, had misdiagnosed his cancer. In his mind, it was an unforgivable mistake. The man was unable to see, however, the price he was truly paying for not extending grace and forgiveness.

It is your life, not your doctor's. Be polite but be firm.

If I had a doctor who had given up on me or misdiagnosed my disease, and I later discovered that there were other hopeful options, I would be angry, too. But as natural and reasonable as feelings of anger might be, clinging to anger simply is not helpful at this time of your life. Anger harbored is even more destructive than hopelessness or

Laughing in the face of death is one of the benefits of being a person of faith.

passivity. It is like a cancer in itself, eating away at your outlook on life and inhibiting your immune system from optimal perform-ance. Your only helpful option now is to forgive anyone who has hurt you or caused you pain. Let it go.

Yes, anger is a God-given feeling that can lead us to correct injustice or rectify unfair situations. But not every opportunity to rectify a wrong is helpful. Now is the time for you to let the past be past and spend your precious time and energy focusing upon your future which, with God's help, will be long and fruitful.

I attended the funeral of a person who had died on the operating table due to complications arising from a fatal deci-sion made by the anesthesiologist. The patient's death was an accident and, of course, the anesthesiologist was devastated. Courageously, he attended the funeral. During the service, the preacher chided this doctor's "stupid mistake." I couldn't believe my ears. It was a wrong statement to make and a poor witness to the Gospel. We have a right to expect our physicians to act professionally but not perfectly. Without some measure of grace, the practice of medicine or ministry would be both unre-warding and counterproductive.

Is there anything about forgiveness that you find difficult to understand? My experience has taught me this: Most people believe that in order to truly *forgive* someone, they must also be able to *forget* the painful situation. This simply is not true. Experiences enter into our long-term memory in one of two ways: (1) through repetition (going over the information again and again until it sticks), or (2) via a highly charged emotion—either good or bad.

For example, you probably wouldn't have any trouble remembering a great meal you enjoyed at an exceptional restaurant or where you were when JFK was assassinated or where you were when the you heard about the *Challenger* or *Columbia* spacecraft explosions. Why do we remember these events? Because of the emotions involved. Because of the *emotional* component, these images become part of the mind's permanent record. There is nothing you can do to make yourself forget those images.

Now is the time to love yourself and others as you've never loved before.

Likewise, there is nothing you can do to make yourself forget an emotionally charged, hurtful experience you endured sometime in your life. The experience will never go away. How can you forget hearing for the first time that you had cancer? The same is true for any highly charged situation in which someone hurt you.

Yet, just because you will not be able to *forget* the pain doesn't mean that you can't *forgive* the offender. Forgiveness is not only wise stewardship of your mind, body, and soul, but it is also your obligation: "Be kind and compassionate to one another, forgiving each other, just as in Christ God forgave you" (Eph. 4:32).

I can clearly remember a situation in which someone deeply hurt me, but on January 5, 2001 at 10:30 AM, I forgave him. My emotional health began to improve from that moment on. If you feel your doctor has hurt you, forgive him or her. If someone else has hurt you and you are burdened by anger, forgive that person, too. Right now, look at the clock. Note the time. Forgive them.

Harvard Medical School offers a continuing education seminar entitled Healing through the Contemplation of Forgiveness. Medical professionals, to be sure, struggle with issues related to unforgiveness. Perhaps they not only see its debilitating effect in the lives of their patients, but also experience its unhappy side effects in their own lives. Here's a Scripture passage worth contemplating:

> Forgive us our debts,
> as we also have forgiven our debtors.
> And lead us not into temptation,
> but deliver us from the evil one.
> For if you forgive men when they sin against you,
> your heavenly Father will also forgive you.
> But if you do not forgive men their sins,
> your Father will not forgive your sins.
>
> MATTHEW 6:12–16

3. COMMIT TO A HOLISTIC APPROACH TO WELLNESS.

I am surprised to hear that some people, much less Christians, need to be convinced to seek holistic approaches to health and wellness. By *holistic*, I certainly do not mean New Age practices or those rooted in Eastern mysticism. I'm referring to the range of valid, complementary therapies that relate to the body, mind, and soul.

Clearly, Jesus included them as tools for healing. Forgiving a person's sins brought healing in some. To me, this points to the debilitating physical effects of guilt and shame, as well as the restorative power of grace. Prayer brought healing to others, pointing to the power of God to heal. Ignoring treatment of the heart, mind, and soul may leave a critically important component out of the healing equation.

I believe that love is the most powerful force in the universe. Those who are raised around hateful people do not thrive, and many do not even survive. Now is the time to love yourself and others as you've never loved before. Take good care of yourself physically, emotionally, spiritually. But use this difficult time of your life to reach out to others as well—to see what you can do to lighten *their* load. Keep in mind that this is tough on them, too. They want to help you but they may be afraid of saying or doing the wrong thing. Put them at ease by talking to them about *their* lives, not just yours. Help *them* laugh. Pray for and encourage them. Think of it: How you handle your battle with cancer can actually be a positive testament to others of God's power and grace. Remember that even the best of friends grow weary of someone who is constantly complaining, depressed, or self-absorbed.

4. WRITE ABOUT YOUR TRAUMATIC EXPERIENCES.

As we have mentioned throughout our visit together, there is a powerful, mysterious correlation between our emotional health and the level of our physical wellness. The more overwhelmed we are emotionally, the less normally our bodies will function.

There is also a correlation between our ability to understand a situation and our well-being. I believe it works like this:

- The better we understand something or someone, the less stress we internalize.
- The less stress we internalize, the better we feel.
- The better we feel, the better our immune system will help fight disease.

Thus, one of the ways we can fight disease is to better understand our past experiences. I have found that writing about them can be remarkable therapy. It helps us to "connect the dots" of our lives. The more dots we connect, the greater our understanding of a situation. The greater our understanding, the more inner peace we feel. And inner peace (instead of harbored stress or unforgiveness) is far better for the immune system we count on to help us fight illness.

Writing allows us to see pieces of ourselves that might need emotional healing so we can experience physical healing.

I regularly teach a writing seminar in which cancer patients are encouraged to write about their traumatic experiences. I have learned that many, if not most, of the patients have endured emotionally disturbing experiences. It is common for them to tell me that "they know when they got cancer." Rightly or wrongly, they often believe there was one particularly traumatic experience that triggered their cancer. Sometimes it was a divorce or other devastating interpersonal conflict. Other times it was the death of a loved one. Yet for others, it may have been the loss of a job. Over and over, patients tell me they know what caused their cancer.

Let me be clear: As of this writing, no one knows what causes cancer. Yet certain observations can be made from which concepts and ideas are drawn. For example, one somewhat controversial idea is called "immune surveillance." This idea has grown out of the observation that our immune systems appear, at times, to malfunction. Why? Well, we've already learned that our emotions and traumatic events often correlate with disease, including cancer.

As the theory goes, our immune systems are like huge radar antennas that, instead of tracking satellites overhead, monitor bodily infections. Radar antennas, once they pick up the signal from the satellite, remain "locked on" until the satellite is beyond range. According to the immune-surveillance idea, our immune systems function somewhat like those radar antennas.

Imagine that your body has thousands of radar-tracking devices designed to track cancer cells and other harmful cells that could lead to disease if left unde-tected. Once the enemy cells are detected by your immune system, signals are sent to your brain, and your body's defense mechanism is employed. All things being equal, your body heals itself. As the psalmist wrote, you are "fearfully and wonderfully made" by God (Ps. 139:13).

The immune system does not distinguish between a flesh wound and an emotional wound.

However, here is an important key: The human immune system apparently does not distinguish between a flesh wound and an emotional wound—*between a cut on your hand and a broken heart*. Either type of wound will garner the attention of the immune system until the pain is healed.

The problem is that many people pay little attention to their emotional wounds. And until the pain is treated, it will not go completely away. "Time heals all wounds" is a nice sentiment, but in reality it is simply not true. Time does not completely heal our pain. Like a bad tooth, emotional wounds need to be extracted by externalizing them—through talking, praying, writing, or even shouting. Unless we learn to deal as intentionally with our emotional wounds as we do with our more obvious physical wounds, our immune systems will likely underperform and leave us more vulnerable to disease. In sum, those who do not deal with their emotional wounds are far more likely to experience sickness than those who do.

Assuming that the immune system does have a "surveillance function," it appears to lock in on the emotional wound (our anger or pain), which diverts it from fully focusing on the cancer. By identifying and writing about your life's traumas, you help your immune system refocus on its search-and-destroy mission with your cancer cells.

> *If ever you have opportunity to let your light shine, it is when you have cancer.*

Write about your life's pain. It's okay to throw the written material away if you want to. Keeping it or mailing it is not nearly as important as identifying your pain and writing about it. You will feel better. You will have more energy to fight your cancer. And it's likely that your immune system will be physically refocused for the fight.

Imagine walking on a tightrope across Niagara Falls, holding on to a long pole for balance. Occasionally, small gusts of wind will unnerve you slightly, but you quickly regain your balance. Now imagine a severe gust of wind—*a wind sheer*—catching you unexpectedly. Down you go! Life is much like that. Most of us adjust easily to the slight gusts of wind we experience in life. And, while some of us never get blindsided by a wind sheer, many of us do. Some people are hit repeatedly by trauma after trauma, all of which have devastating effects upon our ability to fight disease.

- A New York City woman with breast cancer described her "wind-sheer experience" as the cause of her illness. Her son worked in one of the Twin Towers that fell on September 11, 2001. He was missing for a day or so, and she was, needless to say, devastated by the possibility that her son had been killed. There is no doubt in her mind that her cancer is directly related to that traumatic experience.

- A man was sued over a real estate transaction. His wife developed breast cancer. She believes the stress caused by the lawsuit caused her cancer.

- One woman divorced her husband because he had an affair. Following the divorce, he continued to harass her. The trauma of discovering the affair devastated her. She believes the divorce and the ongoing problems related to it contributed to her having developed cancer.

Whether right or wrong in their assumptions, many patients share similar stories in my writing class. And then an amazing thing happens: the pain, rage, hurt, and anger these people have harbored almost always dissipates ... and sometimes completely fades into oblivion. As a result, the men and women are freed

Like Jeremiah, be remembered for your praises and not for your laments.

from their painful past which, in turn, frees their immune systems to look for and lock in on cancer cells. Again, we would do well to heed advice from the apostle Paul:

Therefore each of you must put off falsehood and speak truth-
fully to his neighbor, for we are all members of one body. "In
your anger do not sin": Do not let the sun go down while you
are still angry, and do not give the devil a foothold.

EPHESIANS 4:25–27

5. LET YOUR LIGHT SHINE!

If ever you have the opportunity to let your light shine, it is
when you have cancer. If ever you have the opportunity to be a
powerful witness for Jesus Christ, it is in the midst of your
struggle against this disease.

Why?

You are a far more credible witness to God's love than
someone whose life is disease-free and going well. Who is going
to listen to someone who has never had any problems in life?

Once my wife, Kay, attended a luncheon where the speaker
began by talking about how wonderful her life had been—how
she had traveled around the world, lived in a nice home, and on
and on. After ten minutes of this, the other ladies were looking
at their watches. But then the speaker's story took a turn. She
began to tell how her husband of thirty years had left her. Not
long after that, she had developed breast cancer. Then she lost
many of the nice things she had enjoyed over the years. Now
everyone in the room was listening to her with great anticipation. Why? Because she was now a credible witness! Her life's
struggles allowed everyone else to identify with her. She spoke
not only of her pain, but also of the great resource her faith in
God had been during her difficult times.

You are in a position to exert a great deal of influence for Jesus. As of this writing, I do not have cancer. I have all of my hair, receding though it may be. I am not nearly as credible a witness to the enabling grace of God as you are. Allow God to use you and your situation to give Him glory. As the apostle Paul taught us:

> So whether you eat or drink or whatever you do,
> do it all for the glory of God.
>
> 1 CORINTHIANS 10:31

A nurse asked me to speak to a patient who was proclaiming—loudly—that all she wanted to do was die. All she would say was, "I wanna die! I wanna die!" Her daughter and another family member were in the room when I entered. It wasn't long before the patient began her litany: "I wanna die!"

"Listen to you," I said. "Can you hear what you are saying? When the good Lord is ready for you to go, He'll come and get you. But right now you are making yourself

The "Take Control" script calls on you to virtually take charge of the fight.

miserable as well as everyone who comes to see you, including me. Why don't you use this as an opportunity to praise God for the life you've lived and for every moment He has given you?"

This stopped her—momentarily at least—and her demeanor changed instantly. I don't know what long-term effect I had on her, but I have learned this: Good, decent, committed Christians often need someone to walk alongside them and help them focus or refocus upon what's important. This woman needed a straight talking-to, and I obliged. I hope I got her refocused on God's love and peace. Why make miserable those who are trying to help you? I encourage you to choose to be a witness for Jesus despite your pain.

The prophet Jeremiah is an example of a man of faith who allowed his light to shine. He wrote not only the book of Jeremiah, but also the book of Lamentations. (Notice a key verb: He *wrote*.) Jeremiah had many reasons to be angry. His life had not gone as he had hoped, and he wrote all about it. But Jeremiah is not remembered for his long litany of problems and complaints—legitimate or otherwise. He is best remembered for his faith in the midst of his pain. Contemplate these words:

> I well remember them, and my soul is downcast within me. Yet this I call to mind and therefore I have hope: Because of the LORD's great love we are not consumed, for his compassions never fail. They are new every morning; great is your faithfulness. I say to myself, "The LORD is my portion; therefore I will wait for him."
>
> LAMENTATIONS 3:20–24

You have reasons to be sad, to be angry, and to complain. But you also have a reason to use this time in your life to let your light shine! Let God's love radiate from you. Leave people thinking, *If I am ever in a difficult situation, I want to be just like this person. My, what a wonderful faith!* Like Jeremiah, be remembered for your praises and not for your laments. Let the words of Jesus guide your spirit during these challenging days:

You are the light of the world. A city on a hill cannot be
hidden. Neither do people light a lamp and put it under
a bowl. Instead they put it on its stand, and it gives light
to everyone in the house. In the same way, let your light
shine before men, that they may see your good deeds
and praise your Father in heaven.

MATTHEW 5:14–16

6. PRAY REPEATEDLY, "YET NOT AS I WILL, BUT AS YOU WILL."

"Given the scientific support of prayer's beneficial effects,
not praying for the best possible outcome may be the equiva-
lent of deliberately withholding an effective drug or a surgical
procedure."[1]

This conclusion comes out of *secular* research. If your own
personal faith in God does not convince you of the power of
prayer, perhaps the secular research will. Medical professionals—Christian and non-Christian—are confirming that
prayer matters.

Prayer works. Now more than ever before, you need to pray
for yourself and encourage others to pray for you.

How exactly should you pray for yourself or ask others to
pray for you? Studies suggest that the most effective prayer is
what's called the *undirected* approach.[2] This approach to prayer
resists the temptation to tell God what to do by asking for a
certain goal or result. It presupposes that God knows what we
need in order to be healed. Therefore, our role is to remove our
own wishes and desires and place ourselves before our loving,
gracious God—asking nothing more than for His light to shine
upon us and that His will be done.

The directed approach, as you would surmise, prays for a *particular* outcome. Researchers have found that while both directed and undirected prayer produce results, the undirected prayer seems to be quantitatively more effective, frequently yielding results twice as great as those arising from the directed approach.[3]

As Jesus anticipated His crucifixion in Gethsemane, He used both directed and undirected prayer:

Directed: "Father, if it is possible, may this cup be taken from me."

Undirected: "Yet not as I will, but as you will."

It's interesting to note that, while Jesus practiced and modeled both types of prayer, His clear desire was that the will of the heavenly Father would prevail: "Yet not as I will, but as you will" (Matt. 26:39). God knows the big picture; we do not. He has the perspective of eternity; our perspective is limited and finite. God's will, whatever it may be, should always be the overriding desire of our hearts. Praying that His will be done is the ultimate prayer of faith.

REMOVE THE BARRIERS

When a seed is planted in soil, what does it need in order to grow? Water, nutrients, and light. All things being equal, the seed should sprout and the plant should grow to maturity. What if you planted a seed and then placed a brick near it? It would get less direct sunlight. Place another brick near it, and even less sunshine would be available. As a result, the plant would be stunted.

If what *we* need is the sunlight of God's love to shine fully upon us in prayer, we must be sure nothing interferes with His direct sunlight. Unfortunately, we often place bricks around ourselves, such as:

- the brick of fear
- the brick of worry
- the brick of anger
- the brick of hatred
- the brick of doubt
- the brick of skepticism
- the brick of self-sufficiency (trusting in ourselves instead of in the sufficiency of God's will for us)

Like the seed planted in the soil, imagine God's light shining upon you. Realize that you may have inadvertently placed bricks around yourself that inhibit the warmth and full-ness of God's sunlight from reaching you. Ask Him to reveal and remove anything that might shade you from His love.

When your prayers display an unwavering trust in His will, they also display an unwavering faith in God's big picture. That is the kind of prayer Jesus prayed in the Garden of Gethsemane. "Yet not as I will, but as you will."

Who among us would want to live our lives outside of God's will?

Your reason for hope means:

- Taking control of your own health care.
- Forgiving those who have hurt you, including doctors who have disappointed you.
- Committing yourself to a holistic approach to wellness. God has provided multiple means of ministering to your

physical, emotional, and spiritual needs. Make yourself available to all of them.

- Ridding yourself of anger by writing about your traumatic experiences.
- Letting your light shine. Your situation makes you a credible witness for Jesus Christ. Don't miss this opportunity to demonstrate your faith in His power and grace.
- Praying for God's will to be done and trusting that His will is good.

A PRAYER OF HOPE

Father in heaven, heal me, I pray. Not because it is in my best interest, but because it is in Your nature to do so. For You alone are the Great Physician. Grant me the grace to remain faithful in the face of pain and suffering, nausea and concern. If You heal me, I will praise You. If I am not to be healed, I will praise You by allowing my light to shine until it is extinguished and You lead me to my eternal home. In Jesus' name, I pray. Amen.

---

1. Tim Birdsall in *How to Treat and Prevent Cancer with Natural Medicine*, Michael Murray, ed. (New York: Riverhead Books, 2002), 190.

2. Ibid., 192.

3. Ibid.

Hold On to Hope

BE STRONG AND TAKE HEART,
ALL YOU WHO HOPE IN THE LORD.

PSALM 31:24

Hold On to Hope

One of the greatest challenges I have is helping people face reality. The reality you face as a Christian with cancer is this:

- Thirty-seven percent of all people with cancer will eventually die from their disease.[1]
- Sixty-three percent of all people with cancer will successfully overcome their disease.
- Among those who do not completely overcome their disease, a positive, fighting attitude can help extend their lives well beyond the time they would have lived without that attitude.
- Your attitude and the decisions you make may very well determine which group you will belong to—the survivors or the nonsurvivors.
- God loves you and does not want you to be sick.

I trust that after reading this book, you are encouraged, if not convinced, that there is hope for your ultimate recovery. I challenge you to read more about areas related to your cancer. There are many other important areas that I chose not to address in this little book, such as the importance of diet, exercise, lifestyle, personal health care, and hygiene. Please take the initiative to learn everything you can about how to improve your chances of becoming a long-term survivor.

Finally, each of us will reach the point where serving God is no longer possible. Do not feel guilty if that is where you are in your journey. One day our mortal bodies will pass into immortality. You may become convinced that you will not survive your cancer and that preparing for death, and that which lies beyond, is more important to you than fighting cancer. If that is to be, live out your days with joy and expectation. You can still be—especially now—a positive testament to God's grace if you are indeed approaching your Homegoing.

In providing this book, however, I have tried to be sure that you are asking yourself the right questions. The right answers to the right questions can provide insights to living, as well as strong motivation to respond faithfully to cancer, serving Jesus Christ, and bearing witness to His love.

Be strong and take heart,
all you who hope in the LORD.
PSALM 31:24

---

1. American Cancer Society 2002 statistics based upon five-year survival rates for all types of cancers combined.

YOUR LIFE JOURNEY

A Reason for Hope

*A Guide for Personal Reflection
or Group Discussion*

By Keith Wall

———————❖———————

USE THESE REFLECTION
QUESTIONS BY YOURSELF,
WITH A LOVED ONE
OR CAREGIVER,
OR IN A GROUP SETTING.

———————————————

One wise writer said, "Hope is hearing the melody of the future. Faith is being able to dance to it." This book is saturated with hope and faith—hope that you can defeat disease and live joyfully through the process; and faith that God is powerful enough to heal you and loving enough to walk with you through the journey.

Since you have this book in your hands, chances are that you are in the midst of hardship and struggle. You may be battling cancer or another serious illness, or perhaps you're caring for someone who is. The greatest ally in the fight against disease is, of course, God Himself. And the other indispensable ally is hope. As Dr. Barry says, "Hope is a necessary ingredient in the healing process.... Without hope, our healing is, at best, impaired or delayed. At worst, hopelessness can lead to premature death. When we have no hope for healing, the mind and body react in accordance with our thoughts and feelings."

The questions in this guide are designed to help cultivate and nurture your hope. They will prompt you to think more deeply about the issues raised in A Reason for Hope and to apply Dr. Barry's principles to your particular situation. Use these reflection questions by yourself, with a loved one or caregiver, or in a group setting. Use the space between questions to jot down your responses, thoughts, resolutions, and prayers.

As you work through these questions, may you indeed be filled with the abundant hope that flows from our heavenly Father.

Chapter One
Are You Hopeful?

1. Dr. Barry asserts that there is a close link between hope and healing. How strongly do you agree with this? Why? In what ways can you develop even more hopefulness as you look to the future?

2. This chapter mentions Proverbs 29:18: "Where there is no vision, the people perish." What does *vision* in this context mean? How would you characterize your vision at this point?

3. The author offers the encouragement and challenge to "believe unflinchingly in your treatment decisions, in your medicine and caregivers, and in God's power to heal you if it is His will to do so." Is there any part of this equation with which you struggle?

4. After reading this book, in what ways can you come to *believe unflinchingly* in each of these aspects?

5. What hope do you gain from knowing that God Himself took on bodily form and experienced physical struggles and setbacks just as we do?

REFLECTION FOR CAREGIVERS AND LOVED ONES

What are some specific things you can do to foster hope and anticipation for the person you're helping?

Chapter Two
Are You Afraid?

1. In this chapter, Dr. Barry recounts the story of Jesus calming the stormy seas after His disciples became fearful. Why do we often feel afraid even though we know Jesus is "in the boat with us"? How can you trust Him more even though you experience fear?

2. Dr. Barry states that "being afraid is understandable, but it is not helpful." Cite some recent situations in which you struggled with fear and how you dealt with it. What has God taught you since then that might help you respond differently in the future?

3. The author encourages cancer patients (and those struggling with other serious illnesses) to find healthy ways to express fear. How are you at expressing your fear? Think of at least three things you can do differently, starting today, to better express your fear in healthy ways.

4. Dr. Barry also asserts that experiencing serious illness can stimulate spiritual renewal. Do you feel you are drawing closer to God during this difficult time of your life? Why or why not? In what ways can you better use this time to be more intimate with the heavenly Father? What would you like to tell family or close friends about how they can help you deepen your faith during this time?

REFLECTION FOR CAREGIVERS AND LOVED ONES

The message woven throughout this chapter is that a diagnosis of cancer is not a death sentence. There is significant reason for hope even though the cancer patient will likely—and quite naturally—experience fear. As a friend or caregiver, think carefully how you might reinforce the reason(s) for hope without dismissing your friend's fear or suffering. Ask God how you can help encourage and cultivate spiritual renewal in your friend's life during these challenging days.

Chapter Three
Does God Want You to Live?

1. Jesus said, "The thief comes only to steal and kill and destroy; I have come that they may have life, and have it to the full" (John 10:10). What do Jesus' words mean to you personally as you fight cancer?

2. Many cancer patients Dr. Barry talks with believe, either consciously or subconsciously, that their disease may be God's punishment for some failure or sin. Review John 10:10 above as well as the other Scriptures cited in the early pages of chapter 3. What picture of God forms in your mind as you contemplate these verses? Who originates illness and who heals illness?

3. Dr. Barry points out the lack of integration between spirituality and health care (though, thankfully, the situation is improving). He says, "Here's the inherent challenge: The scientific and medical communities move slowly, and the church often moves even more slowly." What do you think he means by this? Do you agree?

4. Many people, including Christians, rely almost totally on medicine and science for healing and assume that God is a disinterested bystander. Has this been true of you, even to a small degree? If so, is your mindset beginning to change? In what ways?

REFLECTION FOR CAREGIVERS AND LOVED ONES

God wants all of us to live joyfully and abundantly in the time He has given us—whether that be years, months, or weeks. What will you do today to help brighten and enrich the life of the person for whom you're caring?

CHAPTER FOUR
Do You Want *to Live?*

1. How strongly do you believe in the connection between mind/faith (beliefs, thoughts, attitudes, feelings) and body/health (blood pressure, immune system, and so on)? Think of some examples from your own life to support your views. How do you think your level of belief in the mind-body connection may affect the way you're approaching your disease and treatment?

2. Dr. Barry makes this bold statement: "If your mind is committed to staying diseased, your body will likely oblige you. But if you *genuinely* want to be made well, your body, to the extent it is able, will marshal the necessary forces to help accomplish that goal." Do you agree? In what ways might your mind be helping or hindering your healing process?

3. Chapter 4 highlights the proverb, "As he thinketh in his heart, so is he" (Prov. 23:7 KJV). Take a moment to paraphrase that verse in today's language. Now, relate it to the challenge before you.

4. How is *your* mind responding today—right now—to your current situation? One way to shift from despair to hope is to ask questions that lead to positive, life-affirming answers instead of negative, self-defeating ones. For example:

NEGATIVE	POSITIVE
• Why me? • What did I do to deserve this? • Why do I have to go through this awful treatment? • Why bother fighting anymore? • Is this the end? Will I be just another statistic?	• What's *good* about this? • What does God want me to learn today? • How can I use this to become a better person? • How can I be a positive example to those around me? • How can I minister to my caregivers as they minister to me?

REFLECTION FOR CAREGIVERS AND LOVED ONES

This chapter makes the case that attitude greatly influences the body's ability to heal. Cancer can be exhausting and frustrating for caregivers, too, so now's a good time to check your own attitude toward your loved one's situation. Are you patient? Upbeat? Kind? Willing to let your loved one express fear or dismay without minimizing his or her concerns? Do *you* believe your loved one can win the battle, despite what doctors may say? Before your next visit, think of at least three tangible ways in which you can help create and maintain an environment of optimism and expectation.

CHAPTER FIVE
Why *Do You Want to Live?*

1. Dr. Barry says, "Human beings seem to have an amazing ability to *will* themselves to live long enough to fulfill their goals." Do you agree or disagree? Why?

2. This chapter recounts the incident in which the author failed to finish a marathon because he became distracted by a blister on his foot (the blister didn't actually exist). What might distract you from your goal of healing and restored health? How do you want to handle such distractions so you can maintain focus on the goal?

3. Dr. Barry says, "Goals are important, but set the *right* goals." What do you think he means by "the *right* goals"? What are *your* "right" goals? If you have not completed the statement, "I WANT TO WIN OVER CANCER BECAUSE … " take several minutes to do so now, in writing.

4. The ultimate goal for wanting to continue living is to serve God and glorify Him. In what specific ways would you like to serve the Lord—during your fight against cancer, during your recovery, and when you're back to full health?

REFLECTION FOR CAREGIVERS AND LOVED ONES

Recalling a time in which he failed to complete a marathon, Dr. Barry concludes, "But after starting up again, I could not muster the physical and mental strength to finish the race…. Focusing on my pain instead of my goal had depleted me." As your friend fights the discomfort and exhaustion of illness, remind him or her of the marathon story to help stay focused on the goal of getting well. Encourage him or her to complete the statement from this chapter ("I WANT TO WIN OVER CANCER BECAUSE …") and to review these reasons aloud with you every day.

CHAPTER SIX
Are You Willing to Fight for Your Life?

1. Dr. Barry says that for people with cancer, now is not the time to be lazy or passive. To what degree are you passive or aggressive, indifferent or invigorated? Do you suffer from "chronic niceness"? Ask God to show you ways you can become more assertive and strong-willed in your fight.

2. Hebrews 6:11–12 says, "We want each of you to show this same diligence to the very end, in order to make your hope sure. We do not want you to become lazy, but to imitate those who through faith and patience inherit what has been promised." How might this verse apply to people fighting cancer and other tough diseases? Now relate this Scripture to your personal situation: How can your hope be "sure"?

3. Many patients Dr. Barry has talked with did not question a poor prognosis or prediction of life expectancy given by their doctors. Think back on your response to disappointing—or even devastating—news. Does bad news make you want to give up, or does it make you want to fight back even harder? Determine today how you will respond if you should hear disappointing news in the future. (To help you form this response in advance, use the life-affirming questions suggested under chapter 4 to stimulate ideas.)

REFLECTION FOR CAREGIVERS AND LOVED ONES

Dr. Barry points out that many cancer patients become passive about their disease and let friends and family make all the decisions about treatment and other arrangements. Is this true for the person you're assisting? Does he or she suffer from "chronic niceness"? Determine how you will encourage the person you're caring for to take more initiative in controlling the battle.

Chapter Seven
What Can You Do to Help Yourself?

1. In chapter 7, Dr. Barry links the act of forgiving others with one's physical, emotional, and spiritual well-being. Describe this linkage in your own words. Is unforgiveness taxing your emotions, weakening your spirit? If there is someone you have been unable to forgive, ask God to help you forgive that person. Then do it—*right now*. Say aloud, "(Name of offender), I forgive you. Today, I let go of any ill feelings or resentment I have harbored toward you."

2. One of the most common feelings cancer patients express is a "loss of control." They feel as though they used to have control over their lives, but now everyone else seems to be making decisions for them. Is this true of your situation? After reviewing this chapter, determine at least three ways in which you resolve to better "take charge" of your health care and other aspects of your life.

3. One encouragement in this chapter is to seek a holistic approach to treatment, which means utilizing a range of complementary therapies that relate to the body, mind, and soul. Are there treatments and resources that you are not utilizing, even though they may be helpful? What might be restraining you from taking advantage of the full range of therapies? List at least two action steps you will take this week to be sure you're maximizing your options.

4. Dr. Barry uses the metaphor of a seed planted in soil to describe how prayer provides us with nutrients necessary for healthy growth. But we sometimes place "bricks" around ourselves (anxiety, hopelessness, resentment, unforgiveness, and so on) that block the direct light of God's love and grace. Are there any such obstacles surrounding you that may keep God's light from shining directly on you? Ask God to reveal and remove anything from your heart that could weaken the nourishing light He wants to shine on you.

REFLECTION FOR CAREGIVERS AND LOVED ONES

This chapter presents several practical ways cancer patients can help themselves battle disease while simultaneously bolstering their spiritual and emotional reserves. These include:

1. Taking control of your own health care.
2. Forgiving those who have hurt you, including your doctors.
3. Committing to a holistic approach to wellness.
4. Writing about your traumatic experiences.
5. Letting your light shine.
6. Praying repeatedly, "Yet not as I will, but as *You* will."

Do you agree with these ideas? What others might you add to the list? In which of these areas can you encourage the individual you're caring for to become more active and engaged?

For More Information

There are fine cancer treatment facilities in hospitals and outpatient clinics across America and around the world, and many facilities believe in a spiritual connection to physical healing from the biblical perspective. Among such facilities are the Cancer Treatment Centers of America, for whom Dr. Barry serves as a chaplain to cancer patients. PHONE: 1-800-FOR-HELP

CANCER TREATMENT CENTERS OF AMERICA
AT MIDWESTERN REGIONAL
MEDICAL CENTER
2520 ELISHA AVENUE
ZION, ILLINOIS 60099

CANCER TREATMENT CENTERS OF AMERICA
AT SOUTHWESTERN REGIONAL
MEDICAL CENTER
2408 81ST STREET, SUITE 100
TULSA, OKLAHOMA 74137-4210

CANCER TREATMENT CENTERS OF AMERICA
AT SEATTLE CANCER TREATMENT AND
WELLNESS CENTER
122 16TH AVENUE EAST
SEATTLE, WASHINGTON 98122

The Word at Work Around the World

A vital part of Cook Communications Ministries is our international outreach, Cook Communications Ministries International (CCMI). Your purchase of this book, and of other books and Christian-growth products from Cook, enables CCMI to provide Bibles and Christian literature to people in more than 150 languages in 65 countries.

Cook Communications Ministries is a not-for-profit, self-supporting organization. Revenues from sales of our books, Bible curricula, and other church and home products not only fund our U.S. ministry, but also fund our CCMI ministry around the world. One hundred percent of donations to CCMI go to our international literature programs.

CCMI reaches out internationally in three ways:

· Our premier International Christian Publishing Institute (ICPI) trains leaders from nationally led publishing houses around the world.

· We provide literature for pastors, evangelists, and Christian workers in their national language.

· We reach people at risk—refugees, AIDS victims, street children, and famine victims—with God's Word.

Word Power, God's Power

Faith Kidz, RiverOak, Honor, Life Journey, Victor, NexGen — every time you purchase a book produced by Cook Communications Ministries, you not only meet a vital personal need in your life or in the life of someone you love, but you're also a part of ministering to José in Colombia, Humberto in Chile, Gousa in India, or Lidiane in Brazil. You help make it possible for a pastor in China, a child in Peru, or a mother in West Africa to enjoy a life-changing book. And because you helped, children and adults around the world are learning God's Word and walking in his ways.

Thank you for your partnership in helping to disciple the world. May God bless you with the power of his Word in your life.

For more information about our international ministries, visit www.ccmi.org.